CLIMB HIGH TO THE TOEIC® L&R TEST

Masako Yasumaru   Akiko Watanabe   Yasushi Totoki   Andrew Zitzmann   Nanae Hama

KINSEIDO

Kinseido Publishing Co., Ltd.

3-21 Kanda Jimbo-cho, Chiyoda-ku,
Tokyo 101-0051, Japan

First published 2024 by Kinseido Publishing Co., Ltd.

Design: DAITECH co., ltd.
Illustrations: Miyuki Suzuki

音声ファイル無料ダウンロード

https://www.kinsei-do.co.jp/download/4207

この教科書で 🎧 DL 00 の表示がある箇所の音声は、上記 URL または QR コードにて
無料でダウンロードできます。自習用音声としてご活用ください。

▶ PC からのダウンロードをお勧めします。スマートフォンなどでダウンロードされる場合は、
　ダウンロード前に「解凍アプリ」をインストールしてください。

▶ URL は、**検索ボックスではなくアドレスバー (URL 表示欄)** に入力してください。

▶ お使いのネットワーク環境によっては、ダウンロードできない場合があります。

⊙ CD 00　左記の表示がある箇所の音声は、教室用 CD（Class Audio CD）に収録されています。

はじめに

　TOEIC® Listening & Reading Test（以下TOEIC® L&R）は、アメリカの非営利テスト開発機関であるETSが運営する、日常生活やビジネスシーンでの英語力を測定する資格試験です。試験時間約45分のリスニングセクション100問と、75分のリーディングセクション100問から構成され、10〜990点の間の5点刻みで採点されます。1979年に第1回目の公開テストが実施され、特に2000年以降、多くの企業がTOEIC® L&Rのスコアを採用や昇進・昇格の判断材料として利用するようになりました。その動きに合わせて、TOEIC® L&Rのスコアをレベル判定や成績評価に用いたり、大学院の進学要件としたり、合否判定の優遇措置としたりする大学も増えてきています。2022年度の日本でのTOEIC® L&Rの受験者数は約197万人に上り、TOEIC® L&Rへの需要はますます高まっています。

　私がTOEIC® L&Rの講義を初めて担当することになったのは、まさに市場のグローバル化が叫ばれ、それに対応できる人材を求める声が高まり、ますます多くの企業がTOEIC® L&Rのスコアに注目し始めた2003年のことでした。ただ、当時はTOEIC® L&R関連の書籍はそれほど出版されておらず、本物を忠実に再現した公式問題集をとにかく数多く解かせて、出題形式に慣れてもらうのが最善だと考えていました。もちろん、そのやり方はもともと英語が得意な学生さんには一定の効果がありましたが、初めてTOEIC® L&Rを受験する学生さんや、受験の経験はあるものの伸び悩んでいる学生さんには、思ったほど効果が得られていないと感じ始めていました。そんな折、私はTOEIC® L&Rのテキスト出版にお誘いいただき、テキストの作成に参加することになりました。そこで傾向を踏まえたリアルな問題を作成するため、そして講義での指導を充実させるため、実際のTOEIC® L&Rを何度も受験し、データを取り始めました。TOEIC® L&Rは2006年と2016年に2度の改訂を経て出題形式が変更されましたが、以後も内容や出題傾向は毎年少しずつ変化し続けています。今回金星堂で5冊目のTOEIC® L&Rテキストとなる、この*CLIMB HIGH TO THE TOEIC® L&R TEST*「TOEIC® L&Rテスト　高みへのステップ」は、TOEIC® L&Rを実際に何度も受験し、TOEIC® L&Rを知り尽くしたメンバーが、現在の出題傾向を徹底的に分析し、その結果を反映して作成した「超実践的TOEIC® L&R攻略テキスト」最新版です。うまく使いこなして、ぜひ皆さんのスコアアップに役立ててください。

　最後に、本テキスト刊行にあたり、金星堂の池田恭子様と四條雪菜様には根気強く編集作業にお付き合いいただき、並々ならぬご尽力を賜りました。この場を借りて改めてお礼申し上げます。

著者代表　安丸 雅子

本書は**CheckLink**対応テキストです
（チェックリンク）

CheckLink のアイコンが表示されている設問は、CheckLinkに対応しています。
CheckLinkを使用しなくても従来通りの授業ができますが、特色をご理解いただき、
授業活性化のためにぜひご活用ください。

CheckLinkの特色について

大掛かりで複雑な従来のe-learningシステムとは異なり、CheckLinkのシステムの大きな特色として次の3点が挙げられます。

❶ これまで行われてきた教科書を使った授業展開に大幅な変化を加えることなく、
専門的な知識なしにデジタル学習環境を導入することができる。

❷ PC教室やCALL教室といった最新の機器が導入された教室に限定されることなく、
普通教室を使用した授業でもデジタル学習環境を導入することができる。

❸ 授業中での使用に特化し、教師・学習者双方のモチベーション・集中力をアップさせ、
授業自体を活性化することができる。

教科書を使用した授業に「デジタル学習環境」を導入できる

本システムでは、学習者は教科書の **CheckLink** のアイコンが表示されている設問にPCやスマートフォン、アプリからインターネットを通して解答します。そして教師は、授業中にリアルタイムで解答結果を把握し、正解率などに応じて有効な解説を行うことができるようになっています。教科書自体は従来と何ら変わりはありません。解答の手段として CheckLinkを使用しない場合でも、従来通りの教科書として使用して授業を行うことも、もちろん可能です。

教室環境を選ばない

従来の多機能な e-learning教材のように学習者側の画面に多くの機能を持たせることはせず、「解答する」ことに機能を特化しました。PCだけでなく、一部タブレット端末やスマートフォン、アプリからの解答も可能です。したがって、PC教室やCALL教室といった大掛かりな教室は必要としません。普通教室でもCheckLinkを用いた授業が可能です。教師はPCだけでなく、一部タブレット端末やスマートフォンからも解答結果の確認をすることができます。

授業を活性化するための支援システム

本システムは予習や復習のツールとしてではなく、授業中に活用されることで真価を発揮する仕組みになっています。 CheckLinkというデジタル学習環境を通じ、教師と学習者双方が授業中に解答状況などの様々な情報を共有することで、学習者はやる気を持って解答し、教師は解答状況に応じて効果的な解説を行う、という好循環を生み出します。 CheckLinkは、普段の授業をより活力のあるものへと変えていきます。

上記3つの大きな特色以外にも、掲示板などの授業中に活用できる機能を用意しています。
従来通りの教科書としても使用はできますが、ぜひ CheckLink の機能をご理解いただき、
普段の授業をより活性化されたものにしていくためにご活用ください。

CheckLinkの使い方

CheckLinkは、PCや一部のタブレット端末、スマートフォン、アプリを用いて、この教科書にある のアイコン表示のある設問に解答するシステムです。

- 初めてCheckLinkを使う場合、以下の要領で「**学習者登録**」と「**教科書登録**」を行います。
- 一度登録を済ませれば、あとは毎回「**ログイン画面**」から入るだけです。CheckLinkを使う教科書が増えたときだけ、改めて「**教科書登録**」を行ってください。

登録はCheckLink
学習者用アプリが
便利です。

ダウンロードは
こちらから▶

▶CheckLink URL
https://checklink.kinsei-do.
co.jp/student/

学習者登録（PC ／タブレット／スマートフォンの場合）

① 上記URLにアクセスすると、右のページが表示されます。**❶学校名**を入力し、**❷「ログイン画面へ」**を選択してください。
PCの場合は**❸「PC用はこちら」**を選択して、PC用ページを表示します。同様に**❹学校名**を入力し、**❺「ログイン画面へ」**を選択してください。

② ログイン画面が表示されたら**❶「初めての方はこちら」**を選択し、「学習者登録」画面に入ります。

PC画面

③ 自分の**❶学籍番号、氏名、メールアドレス**（学校のメールなどPCメールを推奨）を入力し、次に**❷任意のパスワード**を8桁以上20桁未満（半角英数字）で入力します。なお、学籍番号はパスワードとして使用することはできません。
「パスワード確認」は、**❷**で入力したパスワードと同じものを入力します。
最後に**❸「登録」**ボタンを選択して、登録は完了です。次回からは、「**ログイン画面**」から学籍番号とパスワードを入力してログインしてください。

教科書登録

① ログイン後、メニュー画面から「**教科書登録**」を選び（PCの場合はその後「**新規登録**」ボタンを選択）、「**教科書登録**」画面を開きます。

② 教科書と受講する授業を登録します。
教科書の最終ページにある、**教科書固有番号**のシールをはがし、**①印字された16桁の数字とアルファベットを入力**します。

③ 授業を担当される先生から連絡された**②11桁の授業ID**を入力します。

④ 最後に**③**「**登録**」ボタンを選択して登録は完了です。

⑤ 実際に使用する際は「**教科書一覧**」（PCの場合は「**教科書選択画面**」）の該当する教科書名を選択すると、「**問題解答**」の画面が表示されます。

問題解答

① 問題は教科書を見ながら解答します。この教科書の ⟲CheckLink のアイコン表示のある設問に解答できます。

② 問題が表示されたら選択肢を選びます。

③ 表示されている問題に解答した後、**①**「**解答**」ボタンを選択すると、解答が登録されます。

● CheckLink推奨環境

PC	携帯電話・スマートフォン

推奨 OS

　　Windows 7, 10 以降

　　MacOS X 以降

推奨ブラウザ

　　Internet Explorer 8.0以上

　　Firefox 40.0以上

　　Google Chrome 50以上

　　Safari

3G以降の携帯電話(docomo, au, softbank)

iPhone、iPad(iOS 9〜)

Android OSスマートフォン、タブレット

●最新の推奨環境についてはウェブサイトをご確認ください。

●上記の推奨環境を満たしている場合でも、機種によってはご利用いただけない場合もあります。
　また、推奨環境は技術動向等により変更される場合があります。

公式サイトでは、
CheckLink活用法について
動画で分かりやすく
説明しています

公式ウェブサイト

https://www.kinsei-do.co.jp/checklink/movie

CheckLink開発

　CheckLinkは奥田裕司 福岡大学教授、正興 ITソリューション株式会社、株式会社金星堂
によって共同開発されました。
　CheckLinkは株式会社金星堂の登録商標です。

CheckLinkの使い方に関するお問い合わせ先

正興ITソリューション株式会社　CheckLink 係

e-mail **checklink@seiko-denki.co.jp**

Contents

TOEIC® Listening & Reading Test について

TOEIC® Listening & Reading Test（以下 TOEIC® L&R）は、オフィスや日常生活での
コミュニケーションの場面における英語のリスニング力とリーディング力を測るテストです。
リスニングセクションとリーディングセクションの2つのセクションで構成されています。

Section	Part	問題形式	問題数
Listening （約45分）	1	**Photographs** （写真描写問題） ● 1枚の写真につき4つの短い説明文を聞いて、最も適切に写真を描写しているものを選ぶ。 ● 説明文は印刷されていない。	6問
	2	**Question-Response** （応答問題） ● 1つの質問または発言と3つの応答を聞いて、最も適切な応答を選ぶ。 ● 質問または発言、応答は印刷されていない。	25問
	3	**Conversations** （会話問題） ● 2人または3人による会話と設問を聞いて、4つの選択肢から最も適切なものを選ぶ。 ● 会話は印刷されていない。	39問 [1つの会話に 3設問×13セット]
	4	**Talks** （説明文問題） ● 説明文と設問を聞いて、4つの選択肢から最も適切なものを選ぶ。 ● 説明文は印刷されていない。	30問 [1つの説明文に 3設問×10セット]

Section	Part	問題形式	問題数
Reading （75分）	5	**Incomplete Sentences** （短文穴埋め問題） ●短い文の中にある空所に入る語（句）として 最も適切なものを、4つの選択肢から選ぶ。	30問
	6	**Text Completion** （長文穴埋め問題） ●長文の中にある4つの空所それぞれにつき、 4つの選択肢から最も適切な語（句）や文を 選ぶ。	16問 ［1つの文書に 4設問×4セット］
	7	**Single passages** （1つの文書） ●1つの文書と設問を読み、4つの選択肢から 最も適切なものを選ぶ。 **Multiple passages** （複数の文書） ●2~3つの関連する文書と設問を読み、4つ の選択肢から最も適切なものを選ぶ。	Single passages： 29問 ［1つの文書に 2~4設問×10セット］ Multiple passages： 25問 ［2~3つの文書に 5設問×5セット］

- マークシート方式のテストで、問題は全て英語で構成されています。
- スコアは、リスニングセクションとリーディングセクションそれぞれ5〜495点、計10〜990点の間の5点刻みで採点されます。
- リスニングセクションの音声は、アメリカ人、イギリス人、カナダ人、オーストラリア人（ニュージーランドを含む）のナレーターによって話されます。

本テキストの構成と使い方

　本テキストは全15ユニットで構成されています。各ユニットには、TOEIC® L&Rで頻出の場面を想定した「テーマ」が設定されており、効率よく学習できるように４つのパート（リスニング２パート、リーディング２パート）が配置されています。

　各ユニットはKey Words & Phrases、Listening Build Up と Listening Try Out、Reading Build Up と Reading Try Outから構成されています。Key Words & Phrasesでは頻出テーマの関連語句を音声と共に確認します。Listening Build Up と Reading Build UpではTOEIC® L&Rより少し易しめの練習問題に取り組み、Listening Try Out と Reading Try Outでは実際のテストと同じ形式の実践問題に挑戦します。

Key Words & Phrases

　ユニットに設定されたテーマの関連語句を A B の２段階で確認します。重要語句は目で見て理解できるだけでなく、耳で聞いて理解できるまで練習を繰り返しましょう。

A 語句レベルの英語を見て日本語になおせるか、また、日本語を見て英語になおせるかどうかを確認しましょう。音声を聞いて、英語をリピートする練習も効果的です。

B A で確認した語句を、英文中に登場する形で聞いて書き取ります。複数形や過去形・過去分詞形などの適切な形に変えられている場合もあるので、聞き取りの際に音の変化にも注意しましょう。

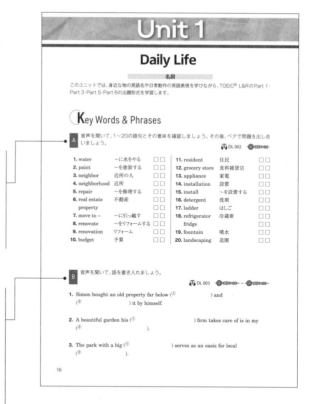

Listening Build Up

各ユニットでは、Part 1〜4の中から2つのパートが取り上げられています。

Point 各パートの解法に関するポイントがまとめられています。

> **Point** 人物1人の写真問題は、動作以後の描写に集中
> 1人の人物が写っている写真問題では、音声で読まれる選択肢の主語が全て同
> ブが約70%を占めます。本ユニットでは1人の人物が写っている写真で、選
> 形の問題を練習します。動作以後の描写の部分に意識を集中しましょう。

Q 実際のテストより少し易しめのリスニング練習問題に取り組みます。音声を聞いて空所を埋めた後、解答を選びます。

> **Q** 音声を聞いて空所を埋めた後、絵に合う説明文を(A)と(B)から選び
> (A) He is (
> (B) He is (

Listening Build Upは、前半ユニットと後半ユニットで問題形式が変わります。

前半（Unit 1 〜 Unit 7）

Part 1	音声を聞いて空所を埋めた後、**絵**に合う説明文を**2択**から選びます。
Part 2	音声を聞いて空所を埋めた後、質問や発言に対する適切な応答文を**2択**から選びます。
Part 3 Part 4	音声を聞いて空所を埋めた後、2問の**日本語**の質問に対する適切な解答を2択から選びます。

> **Q** 説明文を聞いて空所を埋めた後、設問の答えを(A)と(B)から選びま
>
> Questions 1 and 2 refer to the following (1.   ) m
> **W:** Hello, this is Top Housing. I have received the orders I (2.
> last Tuesday. However, I noticed there were some mistakes. I (
> 20 anti-reflective picture frames and 15 photo albums. Actually
> are not included in the (4.   ). I will use them a
> next week. So would you deliver the (5.   ) items
> 1. 話し手はどこで働いていると考えられますか。
>   (A) 不動産会社   (B) 写真スタジオ
> 2. 来週、何が起こりますか。
>   (A) 写真コンテストが開催される   (B) 就職説明会が開催される

後半（Unit 8 〜 Unit 15）

Part 1	音声を聞いて空所を埋めた後、**写真**に合う説明文を**4択**から選びます。
Part 2	音声を聞いて空所を埋めた後、質問や発言に対する適切な応答文を**3択**から選びます。
Part 3 Part 4	音声を聞いて空所を埋めた後、2問の**英語**の質問に対する適切な解答を2択から選びます。

> **Q** 説明文を聞いて空所を埋めた後、設問の答えを(A)と(B)から選びま
>
> Questions 1 and 2 refer to the following (1.   ) from
> **M:** I'd like to start our meeting with an update of the (2.
> products for the trade fair in two weeks. As originally planned,
> with our logo will be (3.   ) out. Next, Mr. Nadler
> give (4.   ) at the booth, but he won't
> If anyone is interested in taking over his (5.   ), let
> 1. What will take place in two weeks?
>   (A) A meeting   (B) A trade fair
> 2. Why does the speaker refer to Mr. Nadler?
>   (A) To regret his retirement   (B) To find his replacement

Listening Try Out

実際のテストと同じ形式の問題に取り組みます。不正解だった問題に関しては、何が原因で正解できなかったのかを分析して記録しておきましょう。

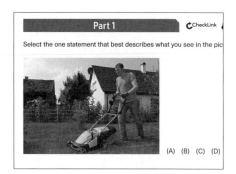

Reading Build Up

各ユニットでは、Part 5とPart 6またはPart 5とPart 7のいずれかの組み合わせで、合計2つのパートが取り上げられています。

Grammar Check　各ユニットには、習得すべき頻出「文法テーマ」が設定されています。空所に日本語や英語、記号を記入して、英文法を確認します。リーディングのみならず、リスニングにとっても重要な文法事項を復習しながら、TOEIC® L&R 頻出の文法ポイントを効率よく押さえていきましょう。

> **名詞** ✐ Grammar Check
>
> →空所に適切な日本語を書き入れましょう。
>
> 名詞は人や物・事の名前を具体的に表す言葉です。日本語の「〜は」「〜が」の「〜」にあたる (1.　　) 語、日本語の「〜を」「〜に」の「〜」にあたる (2.　　) 語や補語、または on the table の the table のように (3.　　) 詞の目的語として使われます。
>
> 英語の名詞は、数えられる「(4.　　) 名詞」と、数えられない「(5.　　) 名詞」に分類できます。数えられる名詞の単数形には、a book のように単数を意味する a(n) が付き、複数形には books のように複数を意味する (e)s が語尾に付きます。
>
> 数えられない名詞は Tom や Japan などの人名や地名を表す (6.　　) 名詞、water などの一定の形を持たない物を表す (7.　　) 名詞、love や happiness など目に見えない概念を表す抽象名詞に分類できますが、いずれも数えられないため a(n) や (e)s は付きません。

Point) 各パートの解法に関するポイントがまとめられています。

> **Point**) 英語の名詞は、動詞や形容詞よりも長くなりがち
>
> 日本語の場合、「学習」に対して「学ぶ」「学習する」のように、名詞は動詞とも短くなる傾向があります。一方、英語の場合、動詞や形容詞に -ion／-ment 付けて名詞を作ることが多いため、install「設置する」に対して installation 詞は動詞や形容詞よりも長くなる傾向があります。

Q　実際のテストより少し易しめの文法とリーディングの練習問題に取り組みます。

> **Q** 文を完成させるのに、正しい語を選びましょう。
>
> 1. All the (residents / resides) managed to evacuate the burning
>
> 2. This town is inconvenient because we have no supermarket or

14

Reading Build Upは、前半ユニットと後半ユニットで問題形式が変わります。

前半（Unit 1 ～ Unit 7）

Part 5	短文の空所に入れるのに適切な語句を2択から選びます。	
Part 6	長文の空所に入れるのに適切な**語句**を2択から選びます。空所は3カ所で、**文補充問題はありません。**	
Part 7	長文を読んで、2問の**日本語**の質問に対する適切な解答を2択から選びます。	

> **Q** 文書を完成させるのに、正しい語を選びましょう。
>
> **Questions 1-3** refer to the following notice.
>
> ---
> **To All Rayleigh Towers Residents**
>
> We have had several 1. (report / reports) that smoke detectors improperly activated. This may occur due to improper installati use of chemicals such as detergents, sprays and paints. To prev alert, make sure the 2. (device / furniture) is installed in the r make sure to ventilate a room when a lot of 3. (misty / mist) i
>
> Thank you for your cooperation.

後半（Unit 8 ～ Unit 15）

Part 5	短文の空所に入れるのに適切な語句を2択から選びます。**※前半ユニットと同様**	
Part 6	長文の空所に入れるのに適切な**語句または文**を2択から選びます。空所は3カ所で、**文補充問題が含まれます。**	
Part 7	長文を読んで、2問の**英語**の質問に対する適切な解答を2択から選びます。	

> **Q** 文書を完成させるのに、正しい語や文を選びましょう。
>
> **Questions 1-3** refer to the following article.
>
> ---
> Cheney's Furniture will extend its business to cleaning service Mike Cheney succeeded his father five years ago. 1. (Over the his skill to restore furniture / The store closed its doors last ye When) he began working, he noticed stains and scratches in t he delivered furniture, and he voluntarily removed them. "Cus me for my work. We should try what competitors cannot do. 3. However), we are adding room cleaning to our services."

Reading Try Out

実際のテストと同じ形式の問題に取り組みます。不正解だった問題に関しては、何が原因で正解できなかったのかを分析して記録しておきましょう。

> **Part 5**
>
> Select the best answer to complete the sentence.
>
> 1. Our community center relies on ------ from many local businesse
>   (A) donate   (B) donated   (C) donating   (D) donations

各ユニットの学習が終了した後も、習熟記録を確認しながら、リスニングの音声のみもう一度聞き直したり、苦手なパートだけを繰り返し復習したりして、本テキストを最大限に活用しましょう。

本テキストの音声データはダウンロードして入手することができます。それらを最大限に活用すれば、リスニング用の問題集を買う必要はありません。音声をスマートフォンや音楽デバイスなどにダウンロードして、毎日1ユニットずつ聞きましょう。授業の予習・復習に役立つのはもちろんのこと、頻出語句の正しい発音や英語独特のイントネーションを浴びて耳を鍛えることで、本番での確実なスコアアップが期待できます。

Unit 1

Daily Life

このユニットでは、身近な物の英語名や日常動作の英語表現を学びながら、TOEIC® L&RのPart 1・Part 3・Part 5・Part 6の出題形式を学習します。

Key Words & Phrases

A 音声を聞いて、1～20の語句とその意味を確認しましょう。その後、ペアで問題を出し合いましょう。

🎧 DL 002 ◉ CD1-02

1. water	～に水をやる	☐☐	11. resident	住民	☐☐
2. paint	～を塗装する	☐☐	12. grocery store	食料雑貨店	☐☐
3. neighbor	近所の人	☐☐	13. appliance	家電	☐☐
4. neighborhood	近所	☐☐	14. installation	設置	☐☐
5. repair	～を修理する	☐☐	15. install	～を設置する	☐☐
6. real estate	不動産	☐☐	16. detergent	洗剤	☐☐
property		☐☐	17. ladder	はしご	☐☐
7. move to ~	～に引っ越す	☐☐	18. refrigerator	冷蔵庫	☐☐
8. renovate	～をリフォームする	☐☐	fridge		☐☐
9. renovation	リフォーム	☐☐	19. fountain	噴水	☐☐
10. budget	予算	☐☐	20. landscaping	造園	☐☐

B 音声を聞いて、語を書き入れましょう。

🎧 DL 003 ◉ CD1-03 ～ ◉ CD1-05

1. Simon bought an old property far below (①   ) and
(②   ) it by himself.

2. A beautiful garden his (①   ) firm takes care of is in my
(②   ).

3. The park with a big (①   ) serves as an oasis for local
(②   ).

Listening Build Up

| Part 1 | 🎧 DL 004 ⊙ CD1-06 ⊙ CD1-07 |

Point 人物1人の写真問題は、動作以後の描写に集中

1人の人物が写っている写真問題では、音声で読まれる選択肢の主語が全て同じ形で出題されるタイプが約70%を占めます。本ユニットでは1人の人物が写っている写真で、選択肢の主語が全て同じ形の問題を練習します。動作以後の描写の部分に意識を集中しましょう。

Q 音声を聞いて空所を埋めた後、絵に合う説明文を(A)と(B)から選びましょう。

(A) He is (　　　　　　　) (　　　　　　　).
(B) He is (　　　　　　　) (　　　　　　　).

| Part 3 | 🎧 DL 005 ⊙ CD1-08 ⊙ CD1-09 |

Point 設問の順番は、音声の流れと一致

基本的に、Part 3とPart 4の設問は、読まれる音声の流れに合わせて配置されています。1つ目の設問の答えは音声の序盤に、2つ目の設問の答えは音声の中盤に、3つ目の設問の答えは音声の終盤に流れてくることが多いです。

Q 会話文を聞いて空所を埋めた後、設問の答えを(A)と(B)から選びましょう。

Questions 1 and 2 refer to the following conversation.

W: Hello. This is Ms. Crandle. When I spoke to you the other day, while you were (1.　　　　　　　) my (2.　　　　　　　)'s home, you told me to call you for an estimate.

M: Yes, Ms. Crandle, I remember speaking to you about your house. I know it's sudden, but does this afternoon (3.　　　　　) for you?

W: That would be fine, but please make it after four P.M.

M: Of course, that's not a problem. I'll come by around four (4.　　　　　).

1. 男性の職業は何ですか。
   (A) テレフォンオペレーター　　　(B) 塗装業者

2. 男性はなぜ女性の家に来るのですか。
   (A) 見積りを出すため　　　(B) 絵を描くため

Listening Try Out

Select the one statement that best describes what you see in the picture.

(A) (B) (C) (D)

Listen to the conversation and select the best response to each question.

1. Where does the conversation most likely take place?

(A) At an architecture firm

(B) At an apartment

(C) At a real estate agency

(D) At a subway station

2. What does the man want to do?

(A) Sell an apartment

(B) Move to a bigger place

(C) Visit a lost and found counter

(D) Renovate a bedroom

3. What will the speakers most likely do next?

(A) Go out to see properties

(B) Inspect a subway

(C) Increase their budget

(D) Revise the bedroom design

Reading Build Up

名詞

Grammar Check

→空所に適切な日本語を書き入れましょう。

名詞は人や物・事の名前を具体的に表す言葉です。日本語の「〜は」「〜が」の「〜」にあたる (1.   ) 語、日本語の「〜を」「〜に」の「〜」にあたる (2.   ) 語や補語、またはon the table の the table のように (3.   ) 詞の目的語として使われます。

英語の名詞は、数えられる「(4.   ) 名詞」と、数えられない「(5.   ) 名詞」に分類できます。数えられる名詞の単数形には、a book のように単数を意味するa(n)が付き、複数形には books のように複数を意味する (e)s が語尾に付きます。

数えられない名詞は Tom や Japan などの人名や地名を表す (6.   ) 名詞、water などの一定の形を持たない物を表す (7.   ) 名詞、love や happiness など目に見えない概念を表す抽象名詞に分類できますが、いずれも数えられないため a(n) や (e)s は付きません。

Part 5

Point 英語の名詞は、動詞や形容詞よりも長くなりがち

日本語の場合、「学習」に対して「学ぶ」「学習する」のように、名詞は動詞と同じ長さか、動詞よりも短くなる傾向があります。一方、英語の場合、動詞や形容詞に -ion / -ment / -ness / -ity などを付けて名詞を作ることが多いため、install「設置する」に対して installation「設置」のように、名詞は動詞や形容詞よりも長くなる傾向があります。

Q 文を完成させるのに、正しい語を選びましょう。

1. All the (residents / resides) managed to evacuate the burning building.

2. This town is inconvenient because we have no supermarket or grocery store in our (neighbor / neighborhood).

3. Some small kitchen (appliances / applies), such as blenders and toasters, are cheaper at that local retailer.

> **Point** パラグラフ（段落）を意識して読む
>
> 各英文を1つ1つの独立したものとして読むのではなく、複数の英文が集まったパラグラフとして読むことを意識しましょう。1つのパラグラフでは1つのトピックが扱われます。そこで話題の中心となるキーワードは、a refrigerator「冷蔵庫」→ it → the kitchen appliance「台所用家電」のように、代名詞や別の表現に置き換えられて繰り返し出現します。

Q 文書を完成させるのに、正しい語を選びましょう。

Questions 1-3 refer to the following notice.

To All Rayleigh Towers Residents

We have had several ¹·(report / reports) that smoke detectors have been improperly activated. This may occur due to improper installation or careless use of chemicals such as detergents, sprays and paints. To prevent a malfunction alert, make sure the ²·(device / furniture) is installed in the right place. Also, make sure to ventilate a room when a lot of ³·(misty / mist) is created.

Thank you for your cooperation.

Joshua Hamilton
Colchester Property Management

Reading Try Out

Select the best answer to complete the sentence.

1. Our community center relies on ------- from many local businesses and organizations.
   (A) donate   (B) donated   (C) donating   (D) donations

2. Ms. Glover asked the vendors to install a new water heater in the -------.
   (A) base   (B) basic   (C) basically   (D) basement

3. Though the average ------- of mattresses ranges from 10 to 12 inches, some customers want one thicker than 15 inches.
   (A) thick   (B) thicken   (C) thickly   (D) thickness

4. Roger leaned a ------- against the house to repair the roof.
   (A) ladder   (B) refrigerator   (C) tutor   (D) commuter

5. The real ------- agency mainly handles rental commercial properties in Brooklyn.
   (A) establish   (B) estate   (C) esteem   (D) estimate

Questions 1-4 refer to the following testimonial.

June 22

Sara Donne

My husband and I were worried about our yard maintenance because we planned to host the 50th wedding anniversary party of our parents there. A lot of debris was scattered, and our lovely fountain was in disrepair. The budget for the repair was limited and the gathering was close at hand. After five companies ------- our offer, I called Anne Landscaping. Anne understood our situation. She
   1.
gave us some ------- and a reasonable price. During the -------, her crew showed
   2.   **3.**

up on time and worked professionally. Although the repair work was temporarily suspended due to unexpected rain, they completed the task before the deadline! The party was a big success. -------. We highly recommend Anne Landscaping, and we will be calling them again.

4.

1. (A) reject
   (B) rejected
   (C) rejection
   (D) rejects

2. (A) suggests
   (B) suggest
   (C) suggestions
   (D) suggesting

3. (A) ceremony
   (B) renovation
   (C) timeline
   (D) campaign

4. (A) The engraved plaque was ordered for the competition.
   (B) Our relatives will help us organize the party.
   (C) We would like to work closely with Anne Landscaping soon.
   (D) In particular, our new fountain pleased our parents and guests.

Unit 2

Eating Out & Shopping

形容詞・副詞

このユニットでは、外食や買い物に関係のある物の英語名や動作の英語表現を学びながら、TOEIC®
L&RのPart 2・Part 4・Part 5・Part 7の出題形式を学習します。

Key Words & Phrases

A 音声を聞いて、1～20の語句とその意味を確認しましょう。その後、ペアで問題を出し合いましょう。

DL 009　CD1-13

1. operation	営業、操業	☐☐	11. serve	～を提供する	☐☐
2. item	商品	☐☐	offer		☐☐
merchandise		☐☐	12. affordable	手ごろな	☐☐
3. order	（～を）注文（する）	☐☐	reasonable		☐☐
4. package	小包	☐☐	13. invoice	請求書、送り状	☐☐
parcel		☐☐	14. exchange	（～を）交換（する）	☐☐
5. deliver	～を配達する	☐☐	15. product	製品	☐☐
6. delivery	配達	☐☐	16. defective	欠陥のある	☐☐
7. purchase	（～を）購入（する）	☐☐	17. out of stock	在庫切れ	☐☐
8. customer	顧客	☐☐	18. subscription	定期購入、継続購入	☐☐
9. recommend	～を薦める	☐☐	19. warranty	保証	☐☐
10. refund	返金	☐☐	20. charge	～を請求する	☐☐

B 音声を聞いて、語を書き入れましょう。

DL 010　CD1-14 ～ CD1-16

1. We don't accept returns or (①   ) unless the item you
   purchased is (②   ).

2. Special Vege's motto is to (①   ) delicious vegan meals at
   (②   ) prices.

3. The product I ordered was out of (①   ) and I canceled the order, but they
   (②   ) it to my credit card by mistake.

Listening Build Up

Part 2 🎧 DL 011 ◉ CD1-17 ◉ CD1-18

Point 疑問詞疑問文の問題は冒頭の疑問詞を聞き逃さない

Part 2 の設問の最初に流れる質問または発言が疑問詞疑問文になっているものは全体の約48%、つまり25問中約12問を占めています。冒頭に読み上げられる疑問詞を聞き逃してしまうと、応答文が全て聞き取れても正答を選べなくなってしまいます。冒頭部分には特に意識を集中しましょう。

Q 音声を聞いて空所を埋めた後、適切な応答文を(A)と(B)から選びましょう。

1. (   ) are your café's hours of operation?

(A) Yes, I (   ) love coffee.

(B) We are (   ) from eleven A.M. to seven P.M.

2. (   ) size do you wear?

(A) It (   ) on the clothing item.

(B) To my favorite apparel (   ).

Part 4 🎧 DL 012 ◉ CD1-19 ◉ CD1-20

Point 導入部を逃さない

Questions xx through xx refer to the following に続く箇所に announcement が入れば「空港や駅でのアナウンス」や「社内でのお知らせ」、telephone message なら「留守番電話」、advertisement なら「広告」、excerpt from a meeting なら「会議の抜粋」、news report や broadcast なら「ニュース」、introduction なら「人物紹介」や「説明」になります。ジャンルが分かっていると心の準備がしやすくなるので、導入部を聞き逃さないようにしましょう。

Q 説明文を聞いて空所を埋めた後、設問の答えを(A)と(B)から選びましょう。

Questions 1 and 2 refer to the following (1.   ) message.

W: Hello, this is Top Housing. I have received the orders I (2.   ) online last Tuesday. However, I noticed there were some mistakes. I (3.   ) 20 anti-reflective picture frames and 15 photo albums. Actually, five picture frames are not included in the (4.   ). I will use them at the career fair next week. So would you deliver the (5.   ) items immediately?

1. 話し手はどこで働いていると考えられますか。

(A) 不動産会社　　　　　　　　　(B) 写真スタジオ

2. 来週、何が起こりますか。

(A) 写真コンテストが開催される　　(B) 就職説明会が開催される

Listening Try Out

Part 2

Listen to the question or statement and the three responses. Then select the best response to the question or statement.

1. (A) (B) (C)

2. (A) (B) (C)

3. (A) (B) (C)

Part 4

Listen to the talk and select the best response to each question.

1. Who is Patricia?

(A) A staff member

(B) An electrician

(C) A news reporter

(D) A customer

2. What problem does the speaker mention?

(A) A delivery is delayed.

(B) Some food is unavailable.

(C) A store is closed.

(D) An appliance does not work.

3. What does the speaker recommend?

(A) Delivering items

(B) Locating a parking lot

(C) Preparing some kitchen tools

(D) Driving on a different road

Reading Build Up

形容詞・副詞

 Grammar Check

→ 空所に適切な日本語や英語を書き入れましょう。

形容詞は人や物・事の (¹.　　　　　) や性質を表す言葉です。affordable「手ごろな」、beautiful「美しい」、delicious「おいしい」、effective「効果的な」のように、-able、-ful、-ous、-ive などの (².　　　　　) 辞が付きます。

日本語と同様に、英語の形容詞にも、tasty tea「おいしいお茶」のように (³.　　　) 詞を修飾する用法と、This tea is tasty.「このお茶はおいしい」のように、動詞の後の補語になる用法の2つの用法があります。

ほとんどの副詞は mainly「主に」や fortunately「幸運にも」のように、形容詞の末尾に -ly を付けて作られたもので、品詞の見分けが容易です。

形容詞が主に名詞を修飾するのに対して、副詞は名詞以外を修飾し、どのように、どのくらいの程度でなど、補足説明をする働きをします。eat (⁴.　　　　　)「ゆっくり食べる」のように (⁵.　　　) 詞を修飾したり、(⁶.　　　) difficult「あまりにも難しい」のように (⁷.　　　　　) 詞を修飾したり、surprisingly smoothly「驚くほど順調に」のように別の副詞を修飾したりします。

Part 5

Point 副詞は置かれる位置にばらつきアリ

形容詞の頻出問題は、〈形容詞＋名詞〉のように名詞を修飾する用法です。副詞の頻出問題は、副詞が動詞を修飾する用法ですが、①〈副詞＋動詞〉、②〈動詞＋副詞〉、③〈動詞＋名詞＋副詞〉など、副詞が置かれる位置にはいくつかのパターンがあります。また受動態の修飾では、④〈be 動詞＋副詞＋過去分詞〉、⑤〈be 動詞＋過去分詞＋副詞〉のようなパターンがあります。

Q 文を完成させるのに、正しい語を選びましょう。

1. Ms. Kirsch had carelessly taken off the price tag, but B&M Clothing gave her a (full / fully) refund.

2. These days more and more people (regular / regularly) purchase organic fruits and vegetables.

3. This cafeteria serves healthy meals and beverages at (extreme / extremely) affordable prices.

26

Point 「導入部→本文の序盤→設問→本文の続き」の順で目を通す

まずは導入部を見て文書の形式をチェックし、本文のタイトルと冒頭に目を通して大まかな話の内容をつかみます。次に設問に目を通し、選択肢は読まずに質問内容だけを確認します。その後本文の続きに戻りますが、設問の順番通りに答えに遭遇することが多いので、どんどん答えていきましょう。設問3問付きの問題は、3分30秒程度での解答を目指しましょう。

Q 文書を読んで、設問の答えを(A)と(B)から選びましょう。

Questions 1-2 refer to the following invoice.

Order Slip

Heron University Bookstore

Date: April 4

Order number: AB5981172

Customer ID: 20220414

Title	Publisher	Quantity	Price
Introduction to Physical Science	Crane Publishing	1	$86.75
Hydrology 101	Orbix & Marx	1	$79.90
Scientific Wonders of the 21st Century	Fortuna Books	1	$48.25
Subtotal			**$214.90**
Shipping fee			$7.00
Discount for first-time order			– $21.49
Total			**$200.41**

Please contact helpdesk@heron-u.bookstore.com if you have any questions.

1. 何冊の本が注文されましたか。

(A) 1冊

(B) 3冊

2. ヘロン大学書店について何が示唆されていますか。

(A) 初めての利用客に割引を提供している。

(B) 200ドルを超える購入は送料が無料になる。

Reading Try Out

Select the best answer to complete the sentence.

1. Cyril sent an e-mail to request an exchange of the ------- product.

(A) defect   (B) defection   (C) defective   (D) defectively

2. The server ------- recommended the most expensive main dish on the menu to us.

(A) strong   (B) strongly   (C) strength   (D) strengthen

3. The item she ordered is ------- out of stock and unavailable, so she has no choice but to cancel the order.

(A) currency   (B) current   (C) currently   (D) currents

4. Almost half of our readers renew their ------- to this fashion magazine.

(A) cashier   (B) patron   (C) subscription   (D) warranty

5. Maggie packed up the merchandise carefully and put an ------- on the outside of the parcel.

(A) income   (B) inquiry   (C) invalid   (D) invoice

Questions 1-3 refer to the following invoice.

Frankie's Kitchens	BILL TO:
454 Airport Drive, Westing, ND 83482	Conrad Marshall
www.frankieskitchens.com	84 Salome Way, Westing, ND
991-723-5224	cmarshall8@usnet.com
	991-587-8351

Invoice No: FK221010
Date of Issue: Oct. 10

Description	Quantity	Unit Price	Total
Removal of old kitchen	8 hours	$55.00	$440.00
Disposal of old kitchen	185 kg	$1.50	$277.50
Installation of kitchen counter, sink, and cabinets	14 hours	$55.00	$770.00
Premium counter and sink (PCS58900)	1	$2,750.00	$2,750.00
Kasput wood cabinets (KWC7501800)	3	$560.00	$1,680.00

Subtotal 1	$5,917.50
Winter promotion 5% discount	– $295.88
Subtotal 2	$5,621.62
Tax rate	8%
Total tax	$449.72
Balance due	$6,071.34

Terms and Conditions

Balance is due within 30 days after the date of issue.

Payment is accepted by cash, credit card, and mobile payment.

Installed products have a 5-year warranty.

You are entitled to a free maintenance check after 2 years.

1. What is true about Frankie's Kitchens?

   (A) It offers special seasonal rates.

   (B) It recruits few experienced plumbers.

   (C) It sells cooking appliances with a 2-year warranty.

   (D) It earned a national reputation for remodeling.

2. How much will Mr. Marshall pay?

   (A) $5,917.50

   (B) $5,621.62

   (C) $449.72

   (D) $6,071.34

3. What is indicated about Mr. Marshall?

   (A) He asked the building contractor to renovate the airport facility.

   (B) He was charged more than the specified total price.

   (C) He will install the whole set of kitchen cabinets himself.

   (D) He can request free maintenance before the end of the warranty.

Classes & Lessons

動詞

このユニットでは、大人向けのさまざまな講座や習い事に関する英語表現を学びながら、TOEIC® L&RのPart 2・Part 3・Part 5・Part 7の出題形式を学習します。

Key Words & Phrases

A 音声を聞いて、1〜20の語句とその意味を確認しましょう。その後、ペアで問題を出し合いましょう。

🎧 DL 016　◎ CD1-26

1. instructor	講師	☐☐
2. take a lesson	レッスンを受ける	☐☐
3. attend	〜に出席する、〜に参加する	☐☐
4. workshop	体験型セミナー	☐☐
5. host	〜を主催[宰]する	☐☐
6. seminar	講習	☐☐
7. (musical) instrument	楽器	☐☐
8. receptionist	受付係	☐☐
9. course	（連続）講座	☐☐
10. enrollment	入会、登録	☐☐
11. trial	お試し	☐☐

12. overtime work	残業	☐☐
13. craft	工芸	☐☐
14. enroll in ~	〜に登録する、〜に入会する	☐☐
register for ~		☐☐
sign up for ~		☐☐
15. pottery	陶芸	☐☐
16. authentic	本格的な	☐☐
17. various	さまざまな	☐☐
18. enthusiastic	熱心な	☐☐
19. publish	〜を出版する	☐☐
20. cookware	調理器具	☐☐

B 音声を聞いて、語を書き入れましょう。

🎧 DL 017　◎ CD1-27 ～ ◎ CD1-29

1. Daniel (①   ) the leather craft (②   ) even after his overtime work.

2. Emily (①   ) in the course without taking a free (②   ) class.

3. The (①   ) said we can experience (②   ) Japanese pottery at the school.

Listening　Build Up

Part 2　　　DL 018　CD1-30　CD1-31

Point　疑問詞疑問文の問題の変則的な応答に慌てない

Who や Whose で始まる疑問詞疑問文の問題では、人物について答えている応答文を選ぶ場合が多いですが、例えば、「この講座の講師は誰ですか」という質問に対して「まだ決定していません」と答える場合もあります。「Who や Whose で始まる質問には必ず人物についての応答文が流れる」といった思い込みを持たない方が慌てずに済みます。

Q　音声を聞いて空所を埋めた後、適切な応答文を(A)と(B)から選びましょう。

1. (　　　　　) is a suitable (　　　　　　　　　) for the piano lesson on Friday?

(A) Katie started (　　　　　) piano lessons.

(B) Jonathan is, I think.

2. (　　　　　) work should I purchase to attend the reading club?

(A) (　　　　) on the list over there.

(B) Mr. Beckman will (　　　).

Part 3　　　DL 019　CD1-32　CD1-33

Point　設問の主語から、誰の発言に意識を集中するかを決めよう

設問の主語を確認し、誰のどの発言に注意するかを決めましょう。例えば、3つの設問のうち、1つ目の設問の主語が the woman の場合、女性の最初の方の発言に解答根拠があることが多いです。

Q　会話文を聞いて空所を埋めた後、設問の答えを(A)と(B)から選びましょう。

Questions 1 and 2 refer to the following conversation.

M: OK, everyone. From next week, we'll be making a replica of a famous fighter jet which (1.　　　　　　　　) in the movie "Top Aviator."

W: Cool! I can't wait! How long will it take to (2.　　　　　　) it?

M: I think we'll need three weeks to build it and one week to paint it.

W: Do we need to (3.　　　　　) our own tools?

M: Yes, please. Don't worry about paint. I will (4.　　　　　　) it.

1. 話し手たちはどこにいると考えられますか。

(A) 工作教室　　(B) 空港

2. 女性は何を持って来なければなりませんか。

(A) 工具　　(B) 塗料

Listening Try Out

Part 2

CheckLink  DL 020

CD1-34 ~ CD1-36

Listen to the question or statement and the three responses. Then select the best response to the question or statement.

1. (A) (B) (C)

2. (A) (B) (C)

3. (A) (B) (C)

Part 3

CheckLink  DL 021, 022

CD1-37 CD1-38

Listen to the conversation and select the best response to each question.

1. Who is the man?

(A) A window cleaner

(B) A receptionist

(C) An instructor

(D) An artisan

2. What does the man ask about?

(A) The woman's preferred courses

(B) The enrollment procedure

(C) The location of a high school

(D) The woman's musical experience

3. What does the man suggest the woman do?

(A) Take a trial lesson

(B) Wipe store windows

(C) Complete her registration

(D) Perform in an orchestra

Reading Build Up

動詞

→ 空所に適切な日本語や英語を書き入れましょう。6と7は適切な記号を選びましょう。

日本語にも「伸びる」という自動詞と「(1.　　　　　　)」という他動詞があるように、英語にも自動詞と他動詞があります。ただし、英語では同じ動詞を自動詞や他動詞として使うことも多いため、動詞単体で見分けるのは難しいです。

自動詞は動作の対象となる (2.　　　　) 語を必要とせず、S+Vの第1文型や、S+V+Cの第2文型の文を作ります。他動詞は目的語を必要とし、S+V+Oの第3文型、S+V+O+ (3.　　　) の第4文型、S+V+O+ (4.　　　) の第5文型の文を作ります。

第2文型 S+V+C のC（補語）はSの (5.　　　　　) や性質を説明する語で、S (6. ＝ / ≠) Cの関係が成り立ちます。それに対して、第3文型 S+V+O のO（目的語）はSの動作の対象となる語で、S (7. ＝ / ≠) Oの関係になります。

自動詞は目的語を必要としないため、直後に前置詞を置くことがあります。一方、他動詞は目的語を必要とするため、直後に前置詞を置くことはありません。

Part 5

Point 自動詞に間違えやすい他動詞を再確認しよう

次の語は、和訳すると前置詞が必要な印象がありますが、全て他動詞なので前置詞は必要ありません。まとめて覚えましょう。
marry「〜と結婚する」、enter「〜に入る」、reach「〜に到着する」、obey「〜に従う」、discuss「〜について議論する」、oppose「〜に反対する」、resemble「〜に似ている」、attend「〜に出席する」、mention「〜について言及する」、approach「〜に接近する」

Q 文を完成させるのに、正しい語を選びましょう。

1. They advised you to take the class on digital photo editing, but you didn't (hear / listen) to them.

2. The new course (gave / presented) me an opportunity to learn computer programming skills from the basics.

3. Her inexperience as an instructor (made / took) her nervous during her first class.

Part 7

Point **ウェブ系の案内やフォームは全体を俯瞰して見よう**

講座の案内、受講の申し込み、講座の感想レビューなどは、ウェブページやオンラインフォーム形式
で出題されることが多いですが、これらは記事やEメールのように「文章を読む」のではなく、どこ
にどのような情報が書いてあるかを「探す」感覚で読むと解答時間の節約につながります。

Q 文書を読んで、設問の答えを(A)と(B)から選びましょう。

Questions 1-2 refer to the following online form.

1. このフォームの目的は何ですか。

(A) 顧客からの問い合わせを受け付けること

(B) 新しい職に就く人材を募集すること

2. このフォームに必ず入力しないといけないものはどれですか。

(A) 住所　　(B) 役職

Reading Try Out

Select the best answer to complete the sentence.

1. It ------- that the level of this violin class is a little high for Nick.
(A) sees   (B) seems   (C) views   (D) watches

2. Deborah had overtime work and didn't ------- the yoga class in time.
(A) arrive   (B) catch   (C) get   (D) reach

3. We ------- the craft workshop for Christmas, at which we made willow stars and wreathes.
(A) attended   (B) were joined   (C) participated   (D) took part

4. Mr. Hammond ------- in the creative writing program, aiming to become a novelist.
(A) enrolled   (B) applied   (C) signed   (D) started

5. A monthly lesson ------- for the pottery class is automatically withdrawn from my bank account.
(A) fee   (B) money   (C) rate   (D) toll

Part 7 CheckLink

Questions 1-3 refer to the following Web page.

https://www.nepalikitchen.com

Authentic Nepali Cooking Classes
By a Nepali chef

If you are someone who likes flavor and freshness, Nepali cuisine is for you.
Through this workshop, you can learn various Nepali recipes
from a Nepali instructor.

Course

Standard Nepali Cooking

1 person:	$84.70 includes 21% tax.
2 persons:	$157.30 includes 21% tax.
3 or more persons:	$229.90 includes 21% tax.

Advanced Nepali Cooking

1 person:	$121.00 includes 21% tax.
2 persons:	$217.80 includes 21% tax.
3 or more persons:	$326.70 includes 21% tax.

Instructor

Raji Prasad Sapkota
Known for world-class Nepali cuisine, he won prizes at the Asian Food Competition of 2019 and 2023 and owns five restaurants in New York.

---

1. For whom is the Web page most likely intended?

(A) People who are looking for a job

(B) People who want to learn a foreign language

(C) People who are enthusiastic about cooking

(D) People who are searching for a good restaurant

2. What is indicated about the instructor?

(A) He has published some recipe books.

(B) He worked at a cookware shop in Nepal.

(C) He is known for world-class French cuisine.

(D) He runs some restaurants in New York.

3. How much is the standard-level workshop for a group of five people?

(A) $157.30

(B) $229.90

(C) $217.80

(D) $326.70

Unit 4

Events

現在形・現在進行形

このユニットでは、パーティーやコンサートなどのイベントに関する英語表現を学びながら、TOEIC® L&RのPart 1・Part 4・Part 5・Part 6の出題形式を学習します。

Key Words & Phrases

A 音声を聞いて、1〜20の語句とその意味を確認しましょう。その後、ペアで問題を出し合いましょう。

DL 023　CD1-39

1. generous	寛大な ☐☐	10. perform	演奏する ☐☐
2. donation	寄付 ☐☐	11. beverage	飲み物 ☐☐
3. complimentary	無料の ☐☐	12. banquet	宴会 ☐☐
4. refreshments	軽食 ☐☐	13. participant	参加者 ☐☐
light meal	☐☐	14. join	〜に加わる、〜に参加する ☐☐
5. award ceremony	授賞式 ☐☐	15. exhibit	展示 ☐☐
6. organizer	主催者 ☐☐	16. celebrate	〜を祝う ☐☐
7. cater	〜に料理を仕出しする ☐☐	17. charity	慈善事業 ☐☐
8. anniversary	〜周年 ☐☐	18. farewell party	送別会 ☐☐
9. be held	開催される ☐☐	19. lottery	くじ引き、抽選 ☐☐
take place	☐☐	20. feature	〜を目玉にする、〜を特集する ☐☐

B 音声を聞いて、語を書き入れましょう。

DL 024　CD1-40 ～ CD1-42

1. Their (①   ) party is (②   ) place in the banquet hall.

2. His jazz band is (①   ) at the 20th
(②   ) event now.

3. We (①   ) the (②   ) ceremony of AF Properties every year.

Listening Build Up

Point 複数人物の写真問題で、主語が複数人物を指す場合は、共通の動作を探す

複数人物が写っている写真問題の約20%は、音声で読まれる選択肢の主語が全て同じ形で出題されます。本ユニットでは複数人物が写っている写真で、選択肢の主語が全て同じ形の問題を練習します。目立つ動作に釣られず、全員に共通の動作を探すようにしましょう。

Q 音声を聞いて空所を埋めた後、絵に合う説明文を(A)と(B)から選びましょう。

(A) They're (　　　　　　) on a (　　　　　　)
    blanket.
(B) They're (　　　　　　) a (　　　　　　) in
    their hands.

Point 最後の設問では未来のことが問われやすい

3つ目の設問で「聞き手は次に何をすると考えられますか」や「話し手は聞き手に何をするよう求めていますか」など、直後の行動について問われることがよくあります。また、「15分後に何が起こりますか」や「来週何が話し合われますか」など、少し後の未来の出来事が問われることもよくあります。いずれの場合も音声の終盤に流れてくることが多いので、逃さず聞き取りましょう。

Q 説明文を聞いて空所を埋めた後、設問の答えを(A)と(B)から選びましょう。

Questions 1 and 2 refer to the following (¹·　　　　　　).

M: Welcome to the grand reopening of the Museum of Medieval Italy. Thanks to your
(²·　　　　　　) donations, this museum has been reopened to the public.
Today Luigi Dovizioso, a (³·　　　　　　) of Italian history, will be speaking
about "Commercial Development in Medieval Italy." (⁴·　　　　　　) that, I'd like
you to go out into the courtyard and enjoy the complimentary
(⁵·　　　　　　).

1. ルイージ・ドヴィツィオーゾとは誰ですか。
(A) 博物館の館長　　　(B) 大学教授

2. 聞き手は次に何をすると考えられますか。
(A) 講演を聴く　　　(B) 中庭に出る

Listening Try Out

Select the one statement that best describes what you see in the picture.

(A)   (B)   (C)   (D)

Listen to the talk and select the best response to each question.

1. What event is the speaker preparing for?

(A) An exhibition

(B) An award ceremony

(C) A concert

(D) A silent auction

2. Who is Ms. Montero?

(A) An event organizer

(B) A musician

(C) A sound engineer

(D) A caterer

3. What does the speaker ask the listener to do?

(A) Play an instrument

(B) Repair some equipment

(C) Cater an event

(D) Read material

Reading Build Up

現在形・現在進行形

→•空所に適切な日本語や英語を書き入れましょう。

現在形は主に「現在の状況」「現在の習慣や反復動作」「普遍の真理」を表します。

be 動詞 以外 の 一般動詞 の 現在形 は、動詞 の 原形 を 用 い ます。ただし、主語 が (1.　　　　) 人称 の (2.　　　　) 数である場合、動詞の原形に(e)sを付けます。

if「もし〜なら」、unless「もし〜でなければ」、when「〜する時」、as (3.　　　　) as「〜するとすぐ」、(4.　　　　) / till「〜するまでずっと」、(5.　　　　) the time「〜する時までには」などの条件・時を表す副詞節の中では、未来の内容であっても、現在形か現在完了形を用います。

現在進行形は〈am / is / are + ~ing〉の形で、「〜している」という意味になり、現在進行中の動作や出来事を表します。また、「〜しかかっている」という意味にもなり、ある到達点への接近を表すこともあります。

現在進行形が使えるのは (6.　　　　) 動詞だけで、have「〜を持っている」などの (7.　　　　) 動詞や、look「〜に見える」などの知覚動詞、like「〜を好む」などの心理動詞は進行形にすることはできません。

Part 5

Point その他の進行形にできない動詞を再確認しよう

進行形にできない動詞は、他にも次のようなものがあります。まとめて覚えておきましょう。
①状態動詞：remain「〜のままである」、belong to 〜「〜に所属している」、consist of 〜「〜から成る」、contain / include「〜を含む」、resemble「〜に似ている」
②知覚動詞：hear「〜が聞こえる」、sound like「〜に聞こえる」、smell「〜のにおいがする」
③心理動詞：want「〜が欲しいと思う」、think「〜と思う」、understand / realize「〜を理解する」、remember「〜を覚えている」

Q 文を完成させるのに、正しい語句を選びましょう。

1. The staff meeting of the Emerald Banquet Hall (starts / is starting) at 8:30 every Saturday.

2. Hundreds of people (attends / are attending) the International Book Awards Ceremony now.

3. All of the festival participants (belong / are belonging) to Kenneth High School.

Point 動詞の時制問題では、散りばめられた時を表す語句を探そう

Part 6 の動詞の時制問題は、空所が含まれた英文だけで考えると、答えを絞りきれない場合があります。空所が含まれた英文の中だけで考えるのではなく、前後の英文、段落全体や文書全体まで範囲を広げて、ヒントとなる時を表す語句を見つけてから、解答を選びましょう。

Q 文書を完成させるのに、正しい語句を選びましょう。

Questions 1-3 refer to the following memo.

To: All Employees
From: Cony Ruto
Date: August 8
Subject: Mr. Crist's Retirement Party

Join us for a retirement party in honor of Dick Crist for 30 years of dedicated service. It ¹·(took / is taking) place at Buono Pizza on Friday at 7:30 P.M. For its ²·(prepare / preparation), I ask you to write your message on the card in the break room. Dick will get a plaque, a watch, and a bouquet as gifts. However, the most precious gift ³·(was / is) an unforgettable party for Dick!

Reading Try Out

Select the best answer to complete the sentence.

1. If you are interested in joining our music event, please ------- to this e-mail by May 20.
   (A) respond   (B) responded   (C) responding   (D) response

2. The summer special event of Melbourne Art Museum ------- a free guided tour for children under 13.
   (A) include   (B) including   (C) includes   (D) is including

3. In celebration of Korean Food Festival, the library ------- a Korean cookbook exhibit throughout this month.
   (A) host   (B) is hosting   (C) is hosted   (D) have hosted

4. We are very proud to celebrate the 100th ------- of our charity club.
   (A) anniversary   (B) diversity   (C) elementary   (D) university

5. We are going to have a ------- party tonight for Emily, the new member to our team.
   (A) reunion   (B) welcome   (C) farewell   (D) retirement

Questions 1-4 refer to the following notice.

Learn Foods and Get Meals

Kevin's Farmers Market (KFM) -------
                                1.
on the third Saturday of every month.
Under the bright sunshine, people -------
                                 2.
their favorite vendors, enjoy talking
with the owners, and buy what they want. Children can run in the fields and join

several games, including a quiz event, a stamp rally, and a lottery.

As the newest activity for kids, KFM will provide a program to learn about different foods. The upcoming ------- will feature dairy products. The instructor Donald Goodman, who is a local cattle rancher, will show them where milk comes from and how to milk cows. Also, they will be able to experience making cheese. -------. Anyone interested in this educational program should meet at 9 A.M. in front of the entrance gate.

1. (A) holds
   (B) to hold
   (C) held
   (D) is held

2. (A) frequent
   (B) frequently
   (C) frequency
   (D) frequencies

3. (A) workshop
   (B) ceremony
   (C) operation
   (D) shooting

4. (A) People visiting Donald's farm used to purchase cheese.
   (B) The ranchers are proud of their products.
   (C) According to the recent study, milk production has increased.
   (D) Finally, they will bake a cheesecake with their hand-made cheese.

Unit 5

Traffic & Travel

過去形・過去進行形

このユニットでは、交通機関・旅行・出張などの移動に関する英語表現を学びながら、TOEIC® L&Rの Part 2・Part 3・Part 5・Part 7の出題形式を学習します。

Key Words & Phrases

A 音声を聞いて、1〜20の語句とその意味を確認しましょう。その後、ペアで問題を出し合いましょう。

DL 030　CD1-50

1. business trip	出張	☐☐	11. leave	〜を出発する	☐☐
2. transfer	乗り換え	☐☐	depart		☐☐
3. delay	（〜を）遅延（させる）	☐☐	12. accompany	〜に同行する	☐☐
4. due to ~	〜のため	☐☐	13. confirm	〜を確認する	☐☐
5. road closure	通行止め	☐☐	14. confirmation	確認	☐☐
6. express train	急行列車	☐☐	15. extend one's stay	滞在を延長する	
7. booking	予約	☐☐			☐☐
reservation		☐☐	16. passenger	乗客	☐☐
8. book	〜を予約する	☐☐	17. public transportation	公共交通機関	
reserve		☐☐			☐☐
9. itinerary	旅程表	☐☐	18. round-trip ticket	往復切符	☐☐
10. get to ~	〜に到着する	☐☐	19. destination	目的地	☐☐
			20. travel agency	旅行代理店	☐☐

B 音声を聞いて、語を書き入れましょう。

DL 031　CD1-51 ～ CD1-53

1. My flight was (①　　　　　　　　) due to the heavy snow, and I couldn't get to my
(②　　　　　　　　) in time.

2. Ms. Sanchez (①　　　　　　　　) her reservation with the travel
(②　　　　　　　　).

3. Julian had (①　　　　　　　　) a hotel room for three nights, but decided to
(②　　　　　　　　) his stay by two days.

44

Listening Build Up

Part 2

🎧 DL 032 　⊙ CD1-54 　⊙ CD1-55

Point Why が聞こえたからといって Because に飛びつかない

疑問詞疑問文の冒頭の疑問詞を正確に聞き取れるようになってきたら、後に続く主語と時制まで意識を集中しましょう。また、Why で始まる疑問詞疑問文は理由を尋ねる疑問文ですが、応答文は必ずしも Because で始まるわけではありません。

Q 音声を聞いて空所を埋めた後、適切な応答文を(A)と(B)から選びましょう。

1. (　　　　　　　) bus did you take to go to the city hall?
　(A) I've just taken a (　　　　　).
　(B) (　　　　　　　) ten.

2. Why (　　　　　) you come to the picnic lunch yesterday?
　(A) Because it's (　　　　　　　).
　(B) I was on a (　　　　　　　) trip.

Part 3

🎧 DL 033 　⊙ CD1-56 　⊙ CD1-57

Point 先読み練習第1段階―設問だけに目を通す練習から始める

ディレクションや設問が読み上げられる間に全ての設問と選択肢に目を通すのが大変な場合は、まずは設問だけに目を通しましょう。特に「疑問詞＋主語＋動詞＋目的語」の部分を集中的に見て、質問内容をしっかり覚えます。意図を問う問題は、セリフの部分だけ見ておくとよいでしょう。

Q 会話文を聞いて空所を埋めた後、設問の答えを(A)と(B)から選びましょう。

Questions 1 and 2 refer to the following conversation.

M: Sorry to arrive late, Brittany. The traffic was terrible.

W: Didn't you come by subway? That's the (¹.　　　　　　　) way to get here.

M: It was a bit confusing with the (².　　　　　　　). I saw that there was a direct bus, so I took that.

W: The traffic in the morning is unpredictable. I (³.　　　　　　　) the subway, as there are no (⁴.　　　　　　) underground.

1. 男性はなぜ遅刻したのですか。
　(A) 渋滞にはまったから　　　　(B) 寝坊したから

2. 女性は何をすることを勧めていますか。
　(A) 前日早めに入浴を済ませる　　(B) 交通手段を変更する

Listening Try Out

CheckLink DL 034
CD1-58 ~ CD1-60

Part 2

Listen to the question or statement and the three responses. Then select the best response to the question or statement.

1. (A) (B) (C)

2. (A) (B) (C)

3. (A) (B) (C)

CheckLink DL 035, 036
CD1-61 CD1-62

Part 3

Listen to the conversation and select the best response to each question.

1. What did the woman send to the man?

(A) A map

(B) A train ticket

(C) A schedule

(D) A waiting list

2. What happened yesterday?

(A) The express train was delayed.

(B) The meeting was postponed.

(C) The man was three hours late.

(D) The woman cancelled her booking.

3. What does the man ask the woman to do?

(A) Place the man's name on a list

(B) Contact Carlson Retailing

(C) Reschedule a meeting

(D) Get on a train to Boston

Reading **Build Up**

過去形・過去進行形

—•空所に適切な日本語や英語を書き入れましょう。

過去形は主に「過去の状況」や「過去の習慣的な反復動作」を表します。

be動詞以外の一般動詞は、動詞の原形に(e)dを付けて規則的に変化する (^{1.}　　　　　)
動詞と、wentやtookのように不規則的に変化する (^{2.}　　　　　) 動詞に分けられ
ます。

過去進行形は〈was / were + ~ing〉の形で、「～していた」という意味になり、過去の
時点で進行中の動作や出来事を表します。また、「～しようとしていた」という意味に
もなり、ある到達点への接近を表すこともあります。

(^{3.}　　　　　)「いつも」や constantly「絶えず」という副詞を伴うと、「いつも
～していた」という意味になり、過去の反復的な動作を表します。非難の気持ちが込め
られることもあります。

現在進行形の場合と同様に、過去進行形が使えるのは動作を表す (^{4.}　　　　) 動詞
だけで、belong「所属する」などの (^{5.}　　　) 動詞、(^{6.}　　　　)「～のにお
いがする」などの知覚動詞、(^{7.}　　　　　)「～を理解する」などの心
理動詞は過去進行形にすることはできません。

Part 5

Point **明確な過去を表す副詞が無くても、過去形を選ばせる問題もある**

TOEIC® L&R で過去形が正答となるのは、文中に yesterday、~ ago、last ~ などの明確な過去を
表す副詞を伴う問題がほとんどです。しかし、そのような過去を表す副詞が無くても、主語の人称・
単複や他の節の時制から判断して過去形を選ばせる問題もあります。

Q 文を完成させるのに、正しい語句を選びましょう。

1. The first subway line (opened / is opened) in Boston in 1897.

2. It (took / was taking) me about five hours to get to Paris because the express
train was delayed.

3. When I talked to my colleague, he (looked / was looking) for a reasonable flight
to Switzerland.

メール文書では件名を見ればおおまかな内容が分かります。また、受信者と送信者のアットマーク以下のアドレスが一致している場合、社内でのやり取りであることが分かります。さらに日付の部分が設問の答えの鍵を握っていることもあります。メール本文に入る前の冒頭部も読み飛ばさずに、目を通しましょう。

Q 文書を読んで、設問の答えを(A)と(B)から選びましょう。

Questions 1-2 refer to the following e-mail.

To:	Catherine Gardner <cgardner@pittsglobaltech.com>
From:	Erick Tucker <etucker@pittsglobaltech.com>
Date:	June 12
Subject:	Our vice president's business trip to San Diego

Hi Catherine,

As you know, our vice president is going to visit the International Trade Fair in San Diego from June 17, but last night she suddenly said she wanted to meet her counterpart of GA Industries while she was there.

I have to leave here today to accompany our president on his trip to Europe. So, could you please confirm and adjust their schedules for me? Our vice president says she'll be able to extend her stay until the 22nd.

I'll come back on the 27th. For urgent matters, please call me at 557-635-1223.

Erick Tucker

1. タッカーさんはなぜメールを書いたのですか。
   (A) ヨーロッパ出張の日程を決めるため
   (B) ガードナーさんに仕事を任せるため

2. タッカーさんはいつ帰ってきますか。
   (A) 6月22日　　(B) 6月27日

Reading Try Out

Select the best answer to complete the sentence.

1. Morgan Ferry safely ------- on Short Island last night.

   (A) arrives   (B) arrived   (C) was arriving   (D) was arrived

2. After a brief check, I ------- some mistakes on the itinerary that my secretary had created for my business trip.

   (A) find   (B) found   (C) founded   (D) was finding

3. The flight was suddenly cancelled due to mechanical problems when the passengers ------- at the boarding gate.

   (A) waits   (B) waited   (C) were waiting   (D) have waited

4. I ------- a confirmation e-mail on my booking for my family holiday.

   (A) received   (B) released   (C) remained   (D) reserved

5. Instead of using public transportation, I ------- a car for a day trip.

   (A) cancelled   (B) delivered   (C) loaded   (D) rented

Questions 1-3 refer to the following e-mail.

To:	Jason Brennan <Jbrennan@webmail.com>
From:	Melanie Finch <mfinch@wondertravel.com>
Date:	May 26
Subject:	Confirmation of reservation

Dear Mr. Brennan:

According to your request, I looked into round-trip tickets to Philadelphia by a budget carrier and the nearest hotel from your destination. I've made a temporary reservation. The itinerary would be:

Depart Atlanta: June 23, 8:05 A.M., F922 Frontier Airways
Arrive Philadelphia: June 23, 10:12 A.M.

Lodging
Location: Sonder Hotel
Check in: Monday, June 23
Check out: Wednesday, June 25
Room: Single

Depart Philadelphia: June 25, 5:20 P.M., F926 Frontier Airways
Arrive Atlanta: June 25, 7:27 P.M.

We have to confirm your temporary reservation by the end of this month, so could you reply to this e-mail by the day after tomorrow as to whether this itinerary suits you? Please do not hesitate to contact us if you have any questions.

Sincerely yours,

Melanie Finch
Wonder Travel Co.

1. What is indicated about Mr. Brennan?

   (A) He wants to travel on a discount plane ticket.

   (B) He will stay with his relative in Philadelphia.

   (C) He works at a travel agency in Atlanta.

   (D) He will go on a trip with his whole family.

2. The word "temporary" in paragraph 1, line 3, is closest in meaning to

   (A) available

   (B) definite

   (C) extensive

   (D) tentative

3. How should Mr. Brennan contact Ms. Finch?

   (A) By calling her smartphone

   (B) By e-mailing her back

   (C) By visiting the nearest branch

   (D) By accessing her company's Web site

Unit 6

News

このユニットでは、ニュースや記事などのメディアに関する英語表現を学びながら、TOEIC® L&Rの Part 1・Part 4・Part 5・Part 6の出題形式を学習します。

Key Words & Phrases

A 音声を聞いて、1〜20の語句とその意味を確認しましょう。その後、ペアで問題を出し合いましょう。

DL 037　CD2-02

1. announcement	発表、告知 □□	10. election	選挙 □□
2. broadcast	(〜を)放送(する) □□	11. disaster	災害 □□
3. report live from 〜	〜から生中継で報道する □□	12. mayor	市長 □□
		13. city council	市議会 □□
4. traffic restriction	交通規制 □□	14. press conference	記者会見 □□
5. make [take] a detour	迂回する □□	15. governor	知事 □□
6. take place	開催される □□	16. according to 〜	〜によると □□
be held	□□	17. weather forecast	天気予報 □□
7. city hall	市役所 □□	18. newsletter	会報 □□
8. venue	会場 □□	19. under construction	建設中で □□
9. latest	最新の □□	20. complete	〜を完了する □□

B 音声を聞いて、語を書き入れましょう。

DL 038　CD2-03 ～ CD2-05

1. (① _____) to the article, the bridge construction will be
   (② _____) soon.

2. (① _____) Blake is having a press (② _____) this
   afternoon.

3. The (① _____) traffic update says the highway is scheduled to be closed from
   5 P.M., so we will have to make a (② _____).

Listening Build Up

Point 人物1人の写真問題でも、主語の聞き取りが必要な問題がある

1人の人物が写っている写真問題では、音声で読まれる選択肢の主語が全て同じ形で出題されるタイプが約70%を占めますが、残りの約30%は4つの選択肢のうち2つの主語が同じ形で出題されています。本ユニットでは1人の人物が写っている写真で、選択肢の主語が2つ同じ形の問題を練習します。油断して主語を聞き逃すことがないように気を付けましょう。

Q 音声を聞いて空所を埋めた後、絵に合う説明文を(A)と(B)から選びましょう。

(A) (　　　　　　　　　　　　　　) are being
　　(　　　　) up on the desk.
(B) He's (　　　　　　) an
　　(　　　　　　　　　　　　).

Point 先読み練習第2段階—頻出の設問は瞬時に理解できるようにする

Where is the speaker?「話し手はどこにいますか」などの場面設定や職場を問う問題、またはWho most likely is the speaker?「話し手は誰だと考えられますか」などの話し手や聞き手の職業を問う問題が1つ目の設問に設定されているパターンは頻出です。見て瞬時に理解できるように練習しましょう。

Q 説明文を聞いて空所を埋めた後、設問の答えを(A)と(B)から選びましょう。

Questions 1 and 2 refer to the following (¹·　　　　　　　　　　).

W: Good afternoon, this is Deanna Milton from WCR (²·　　　　　　), reporting
(³·　　　　) from South Valley Mall, where the staff are busy preparing for its
grand (⁴·　　　　　　) tomorrow. Any shopper who comes tomorrow will
get a shopping bag only (⁵·　　　　　　　　) on the opening day. You should
definitely come here tomorrow for the grand opening!

1. 話し手の勤務先はどこですか。
　(A) ラジオ局　　　　　　　　(B) ショッピングモール

2. 無料のショッピングバッグをもらうには、聞き手はどうしたらよいですか。
　(A) 50ドル以上の食事をする　　(B) 初日に来る

Listening Try Out

Select the one statement that best describes what you see in the picture.

(A) (B) (C) (D)

Listen to the talk and select the best response to each question.

1. Who is the speaker?

(A) A newscaster

(B) A marathon runner

(C) A traffic controller

(D) An event organizer

2. What can listeners find on a Web site?

(A) An entry form

(B) An event schedule

(C) A list of official sponsors

(D) A map of traffic restrictions

3. What does the speaker suggest?

(A) Entering a competition

(B) Making a detour

(C) Serving as a volunteer

(D) Donating to a charity

Reading Build Up

未来表現

→空所に適切な英語を書き入れましょう。

〈助動詞の（1.　　　　　　）＋動詞の原形〉で、単純未来や未来推量「〜だろう」、その場で決定した意志「〜するつもりだ」など、未来のことを表します。

現在進行形やbe going to do を使うと、すでに確定した未来や予定を表すことができます。「私は明日、エミリーと会う予定です」を英語で表す際、現在進行形を使って "(2.　　　　　)(3.　　　　　　　　　) Emily tomorrow."、またはbe going to do を使って "(4.　　　　　) going to (5.　　　　　　) Emily tomorrow." と表現できますが、微妙な違いがあります。現在進行形の文は、会うことが決定しているだけでなく、すでにスケジュールの調整や手配まで済んでいることを表します。一方、be going to do を使った文は、すでに会うことは決定しているものの、具体的な調整はまだ行われていないことを意味します。

その他の予想・予定・意志を意味する表現に、be (6.　　　　　　　) to do「〜しそうだ」、be expected to do「〜することが見込まれている」、be planning to do「〜する予定だ」、be scheduled to do「〜する予定だ」、be (7.　　　　　　　　　) to do「〜することになっている」、intend to do「〜するつもりだ」、expect to do「〜すると予想する、〜するつもりだ」などがあります。

Part 5

Point 未来の表現と共に使われる副詞を再確認しよう

未来を表す表現は tomorrow「明日」、the day after tomorrow「明後日」、next week「来週」、soon「もうすぐ」、from now (on)「今後ずっと」などの未来を表す語（句）と共によく用いられます。

Q 文を完成させるのに、正しい語句を選びましょう。

1. The latest weather news says we (have / will have) heavy rain tomorrow.

2. Kingsbridge Community Center (reopening / is reopening) next Saturday.

3. The next mayoral election (will schedule / is scheduled) to be held in three years.

Part 6

語彙問題は、前後の英文と関連がある語句を選ぶ

Part 6 の語彙問題では、前後の英文や段落全体まで確認する範囲を広げて、つながりを意識した語句を選びましょう。redo tiles「タイルを貼り替える」、paint walls「壁を塗る」などが散りばめられている文の前後で、refurbishment「改装」を選ばなければならないといった、内容に関連した語句が正答となる語彙問題はよく出題されています。

Q 文書を完成させるのに、正しい語句を選びましょう。

Questions 1-3 refer to the following article.

Record Rain Strands 250 Passengers at Kannur Airport

Kerala, a city in the south of India, 1. (experiencing / is experiencing)
unprecedented rainfall. Severe floods washed out highways and houses there.
The runway at Kannur Airport was also flooded. All 2. (flights / conferences)
were cancelled, and 250 passengers and staff are urged to stay there. The rain is
expected to continue over the next few days. The rescue teams 3. (will not reach
/ did not reach) the disaster areas until the rain stops.

Reading Try Out

Select the best answer to complete the sentence.

1. Mayor Karen Dickens has announced that she ------- re-election for the upcoming mayoral race.

(A) seek   (B) will seek   (C) were seeking   (D) has never sought

2. The CBK news reports that the city council election ------- place in two days.

(A) take   (B) taken   (C) is taking   (D) have taken

3. LBS, one of the local TV stations, ------- to broadcast a press conference by Governor Mike Rogers next Monday.

(A) suppose   (B) supposing   (C) supposed   (D) is supposed

4. Residents in the neighborhood will need to take a ------- as the main street has road maintenance scheduled for this weekend.

(A) decorate   (B) deliver   (C) detour   (D) develop

5. According to the weather -------, the weather here is expected to remain cold and rainy for the next 24 hours.

(A) forecast   (B) nationwide   (C) spokesperson   (D) formula

Questions 1-4 refer to the following newsletter.

New University President

Chelmsford University's presidential election was held on 11 November. The incumbent President Dr. Jonathan Palin was term-limited and ineligible to run for re-election. Dr. Serena Morton was ------- as the first female president of
1.
Chelmsford University.

"I am extremely proud to take over Jonathan's ------. Jonathan accomplished great
2.
achievements. First of all, under his management, we are in the top 20 in terms

of academic research. Moreover, he started generous scholarship programs,

which attract many talented students. As a result, we have been producing

famous alumni in several fields. ------. He succeeded in raising enough donations
3.
to build a new research facility. Now our new facility is under construction in

the southern part of the campus, and ------ completed next summer," said Dr.
4.
Morton.

She will take the post of President in January next year, serving a five-year term.

1. (A) elect
   (B) elected
   (C) electing
   (D) election

2. (A) lectures
   (B) availability
   (C) clothes
   (D) responsibilities

3. (A) His last contribution is still in progress.
   (B) Their research is on the second phase.
   (C) They are expected to have plenty of funds.
   (D) Therefore, he will resign his duties at the end of January.

4. (A) was
   (B) have been
   (C) will be
   (D) are

Unit 7

Job Offers & Employment

現在完了形

このユニットでは、就職活動・求人・採用に関する英語表現を学びながら、TOEIC® L&RのPart 2・Part 3・Part 5・Part 7の出題形式を学習します。

Key Words & Phrases

A 音声を聞いて、1〜20の語句とその意味を確認しましょう。その後、ペアで問題を出し合いましょう。

⬇ DL 044   ◉ CD2-13

1. recruit	新入社員	10. HR (human resources) personnel	人事
2. recruiter	人材採用担当者	11. orientation	新入社員向け説明会
3. job fair	就職説明会	12. position	（役）職
4. apply to（申請先） apply for（目的）	〜に応募する	13. submit	〜を提出する
5. applicant	応募者	14. interview	面接
6. company corporation firm	会社、企業	15. job-hunt	就職活動をする
		16. job opening vacancy	求人、欠員
7. portfolio	ポートフォリオ、作品集	17. attach	〜を添付する
8. internship	実務研修	18. candidate	候補者
9. résumé CV (curriculum vitae)	履歴書	19. proficiency	熟練、堪能
		20. fluent	流暢な

B 音声を聞いて、語を書き入れましょう。

⬇ DL 045   ◉ CD2-14 ～ ◉ CD2-16

1. Most of the (① _____) at the job fair have taken part in the
   (② _____) of their first-choice company before.

2. Christine has (① _____) a résumé to eight
   (② _____) so far.

3. The (① _____) manager has been in charge of (② _____) for the
   past three years.

Listening Build Up

Part 2

Point) Where と When の聞き取りに注意

疑問詞疑問文の疑問詞 Where と When は出だしの音が似ている上、どちらも冒頭で読まれると聞き取りづらいので要注意です。

Q 音声を聞いて空所を埋めた後、適切な応答文を (A) と (B) から選びましょう。

1. (　　　　　　) can I find the list of recruits?
  (A) I saw it (　　　) the manager's desk.
  (B) At a (　　　　　　) past eleven A.M.

2. (　　　　　) can you start to work?
  (A) I have just (　　　　　　　) around the office.
  (B) I (　　　) start right away.

Part 3

Point) 先読み練習第3段階—設問に加えて選択肢にも目を通す

余裕が出てきたら、短い選択肢まで目を通す範囲を広げましょう。例えば、1つ目の「何が問題か」という設問の選択肢が「資料が見当たらない」「進行が遅れている」「会議に間に合わない」「装置が作動しない」、2つ目の「男性が女性に望むことは何か」という設問の選択肢が「文書を添付する」「残業する」「シフトを替わる」「業者に電話する」である場合、トラブルで困っている男性と同僚の女性との会話だと予想できます。

Q 会話文を聞いて空所を埋めた後、設問の答えを (A) と (B) から選びましょう。

Questions 1 and 2 refer to the following conversation.

W: This job fair is very popular. Did you say that you would (1.　　　　　　) to Meta Creative Studio? Their booth was really crowded.

M: That's not surprising. It's a popular graphic design company. Of course, I have my application and (2.　　　　　　) with me, but I have no confidence.

W: Feel positive. You did an (3.　　　　　　) with them, didn't you?

M: I did. OK, I'll go talk with the (4.　　　　　　).

1. 話し手たちはどこにいますか。
  (A) メタ・クリエイティブ・スタジオ   (B) 就職説明会

2. 男性は次に何をすると言っていますか。
  (A) 担当者と話をする   (B) 実務研修に参加する

Listening Try Out

Listen to the question or statement and the three responses. Then select the best response to the question or statement.

1. (A) (B) (C)

2. (A) (B) (C)

3. (A) (B) (C)

Listen to the conversation and select the best response to each question.

1. Where is the conversation most likely taking place?

(A) In a TV studio

(B) In a university classroom

(C) In an unemployment office

(D) In an interview room

2. According to the man, what is special about the company?

(A) It is a fast-growing startup.

(B) It has good working conditions.

(C) It is located near his university.

(D) It has a high ratio of part-time workers.

3. What is the man concerned about?

(A) How the company will let him know the result of the interview

(B) When he will start working at a new branch

(C) Whether he can choose his workplace location

(D) What forms the company requires him to submit

Reading Build Up

現在完了形

・空所に適切な日本語や英語を書き入れましょう。

現在完了形は〈have / has + 過去分詞〉の形で表され、完了・結果「～してしまった」「～したところだ」、経験「～したことがある」、継続「ずっと～している」の意味を持っています。

完了・結果「～してしまった」「～したところだ」は、already「すでに、もう」、(1.　　　　　)「因まだ、麗もう」、(2.　　　　　)「ちょうど」などの副詞を伴うことが多いです。

経験「～したことがある」は、ever「今までに」、(3.　　　　　)「一度も～ない」、(4.　　　　　)「かつて、一度」、before「以前」などの回数を表す語を伴うことが多いです。

状態動詞を用いた状態の継続「ずっと～している」は〈have / has + 過去分詞〉の現在完了形で表しますが、動作動詞を用いた動作の継続「ずっと～し続けている」は〈have / has + been + ~ing〉の (5.　　　　　　　) 形で表します。どちらも、前置詞 (6.　　　　) 「～の間」や接続詞・前置詞 (7.　　　　　) 「～以来」を伴うことが多いです。

Part 5

Point　現在完了形と共に使えない語（句）を再確認しよう

yesterday、then、~ ago、last ~ などの明確な過去を表す副詞は、単体では現在完了形と共に使うことができません。文中で使われている、時制に関わる語（句）をよく確認して、適切な時制を考えましょう。

Q 文を完成させるのに、正しい語句を選びましょう。

1. I totally forgot about it, but the deadline for applications (have / has) already passed.

2. Kate (has / has had) job interviews with the aviation industry several times.

3. Antonio has been (job-hunted / job-hunting) for three months.

Point) 鉄板の流れを理解して、情報をつかみ取ろう

求人情報は、職務内容、応募資格、応募方法の順番で情報が配置されることが多く、展開がほぼ決まっています。また、採用通知には採用された人への指示が含まれ、その理解度を問う問題が出題されます。設問の先読みを徹底して、人名や日付、場所などの細かい情報を見逃さないようにしましょう。

Q 文書を読んで、設問の答えを(A)と(B)から選びましょう。

Questions 1-2 refer to the following e-mail.

To:	All Art Students
From:	Sally Fisher
Date:	Wednesday, June 20
Subject:	Temporary Workers Wanted

Dear Students,

Jelletty Museum is going to have a special exhibition of Italian oil paintings starting in early September. They are seeking some energetic student workers to help out. The work assignment is for three months. Applicants must be familiar with 19th century Italian art. Also, you must work four days a week. Interested students should apply for the position through the museum's Web site by the end of July.

Sally Fisher
Professor of Italian Art History

1. 応募者はどのような要件を求められていますか。

(A) 専門分野の知識　　　(B) 美術館で働いた経験

2. どのようにして応募したらよいですか。

(A) メールに返信する　　(B) ウェブサイトを利用する

Reading Try Out

Part 5

Select the best answer to complete the sentence.

1. There are too many applicants for the position, so we ------- finished looking over all of their CVs yet.

(A) don't   (B) didn't   (C) haven't   (D) hadn't

2. Ms. Park isn't going to apply for the job opening at the law firm because she heard they don't employ those who have ------- its internship program.

(A) not join   (B) never joined   (C) not to joining   (D) never to join

3. Our team has been ------- material for the new employee orientation since this morning.

(A) prepare   (B) prepared   (C) preparation   (D) preparing

4. Briggs & Steinborn, Inc. required him to ------- his résumé and cover letter as PDFs to the e-mail.

(A) achieve   (B) analyze   (C) assign   (D) attach

5. The candidate has a high score in the Spanish written proficiency test, but she isn't a ------- speaker.

(A) fluent   (B) knowledge   (C) portfolio   (D) temporary

Part 7

Questions 1-3 refer to the following e-mail.

To:	Roger Wells
From:	Ellen Sandel
Date:	Friday, September 19
Subject:	First Meeting

Dear Mr. Wells,

Thank you very much for your application. We were very impressed with your Japanese-style garden plan using local plants, so we decided to offer you the position of garden designer for our new hotel in Seattle. As you know, we have several hotels in Asian countries, but it is the first time to expand our business into the U.S. We are very proud of having an opportunity to work with you.

Before starting the construction project, we would like to meet with you on October 1 or 2 at our Tokyo office. Are you available on either day? If it is difficult for you to come to our office, we would be very happy to have an online meeting. Please let us know the best date and way to talk with you.

Our president, Kosuke Tanahashi, is excited to see you. He is familiar with your previous works, and he knows quite well how brilliant they are.

Sincerely,

Ellen Sandel
Sunset Hotel Group

1. Who is Mr. Wells?

(A) A hotel receptionist

(B) A construction manager

(C) A landscaper

(D) A president of a company

2. What is true about Sunset Hotel Group?

(A) It is an international company.

(B) It has an office in the U.S.

(C) It has several hotels in Seattle.

(D) It was designed by Mr. Tanahashi.

3. Why is Mr. Tanahashi excited?

(A) He is moving to Seattle.

(B) He gets an opportunity to meet Mr. Wells.

(C) He is going to get an interview online.

(D) He can work with Mr. Wells in the U.S. again.

Unit 8

Office Work & Meetings

受動態

このユニットでは、企画・マーケティング・会議・備品管理などの社内業務に関する英語表現を学びながら、TOEIC® L&RのPart 2・Part 4・Part 5・Part 7の出題形式を学習します。

Key Words & Phrases

A 音声を聞いて、1〜20の語句とその意味を確認しましょう。その後、ペアで問題を出し合いましょう。

DL 051　CD2-26

1. behind schedule　予定より遅れて □□
2. copy machine　コピー機 □□
   (photo)copier □□
3. update　最新情報 □□
4. give a presentation　プレゼンする □□
5. input　　　（〜を）入力（する）□□
6. office supplies　事務用品 □□
7. manager　部長 □□
8. potential customer　潜在顧客 □□
9. approval　承認 □□
10. agenda　議題 □□

11. subordinate　部下 □□
12. strategy　戦略 □□
13. document　文書 □□
14. distribute　〜を配布する □□
15. colleague　同僚 □□
    coworker □□
16. survey　アンケート調査 □□
17. sales representative　営業担当者 □□
18. submission　提出 □□
19. proposal　企画書 □□
20. client　顧客、取引先 □□

B 音声を聞いて、語を書き入れましょう。

DL 052　CD2-27 〜 CD2-29

1. (① 　　　　　　) work of the (② 　　　　　　) results has been finished.

2. A wide range of office (① 　　　　　　) including (② 　　　　　　) paper are sold at Max Stationery.

3. Our top sales (① 　　　　　　) was asked to give a (② 　　　　　　) at the upcoming trade fair.

Listening Build Up

Part 2

🎧 DL 053 ◎ CD2-30 ◎ CD2-31

> **Point** How ＋ 形容詞／副詞に慣れよう

疑問詞 How を単独で使用すると、「どのような」と様子を尋ねたり、「どのようにして」と方法を尋ねたりする疑問詞疑問文となりますが、How ＋ many で人数や個数を、How ＋ often で頻度を、How ＋ long で長さを尋ねる疑問詞疑問文となります。

Q 音声を聞いて空所を埋めた後、適切な応答文を (A) 〜 (C) から選びましょう。

1. How is the (　　　　　) going?

  (A) Unfortunately, it's behind (　　　　　　　).

  (B) (　　　) train.

  (C) It's very (　　　　　　) and creamy.

2. How (　　　　　) is the copy machine maintained?

  (A) (　　　) a few weeks.

  (B) It wasn't (　　　　　　　　　) a decade ago.

  (C) Maybe (　　　　　　).

Part 4

🎧 DL 054, 055 ◎ CD2-32 〜 ◎ CD2-34

> **Point** 先読み練習第4段階—先読み練習の仕上げ

設問と短い選択肢まで読めるようになったら、文章になっている長い選択肢も含めて、設問と選択肢全てに目を通します。情報量が多ければ多いほど、場面設定や話の展開を一層予想しやすくなるので、反応速度と正解率が上がります。

Q 説明文を聞いて空所を埋めた後、設問の答えを (A) と (B) から選びましょう。

Questions 1 and 2 refer to the following (**1.**　　　　　　　) from a meeting.

M: I'd like to start our meeting with an update of the (**2.**　　　　　　　　　　)
products for the trade fair in two weeks. As originally planned, tote bags imprinted
with our logo will be (**3.**　　　　　　) out. Next, Mr. Nadler was supposed to
give (**4.**　　　　　　　　) at the booth, but he won't be able to make it.
If anyone is interested in taking over his (**5.**　　　　　　), let me know.

1. What will take place in two weeks?

  (A) A meeting   (B) A trade fair

2. Why does the speaker refer to Mr. Nadler?

  (A) To regret his retirement   (B) To find his replacement

Listening Try Out

Part 2	CheckLink DL 056 CD2-35 ~ CD2-37

Listen to the question or statement and the three responses. Then select the best response to the question or statement.

1. (A) (B) (C)
2. (A) (B) (C)
3. (A) (B) (C)

Part 4	CheckLink DL 057, 058 CD2-38 CD2-39

Listen to the talk and select the best response to each question.

1. What does the speaker say about the procedure for ordering office supplies?
   (A) It has been abolished.
   (B) It needs permission from the stockholders.
   (C) It is highly evaluated.
   (D) It has been changed.

2. Who are the listeners?
   (A) New employees
   (B) Office supply vendors
   (C) Managers
   (D) Potential customers

3. According to the speaker, what is on a Web site?
   (A) An order form
   (B) Contact information
   (C) A discount coupon
   (D) A promotional video

Reading Build Up

受動態

・空所に適切な日本語や英語を書き入れましょう。

受動態の基本形は〈be動詞＋ (¹.   )〉で、「～（ら）れる」「～（ら）れている」という受け身の意味を表します。動作主が前置詞 (².   ) の後ろに置かれることもあります。

動作主を表す際に by 以外の前置詞を使うものには、be covered (³.   ) ～「～に覆われている」、be known (⁴.   ) ～「～に知られている」、be interested (⁵.   ) ～「～に興味がある」などがあります。

助動詞の後ろは動詞の原形になるので、助動詞を伴う受動態は、〈助動詞＋ be ＋過去分詞〉の形になります。

現在進行形の受動態は〈am / is / are ＋ (⁶.   ) ＋過去分詞〉の形で表され、「～されている最中だ」「～されつつある」の意味になります。現在完了形の受動態は〈have / has ＋ (⁷.   ) ＋過去分詞〉の形で表され、「～されてきた」「～されてしまった」などの意味になります。

Part 5

Point 受動態か進行形か

〈be 動詞＋ ~ing〉で〈進行形〉にするか、〈be 動詞＋過去分詞〉で〈受動態〉にするかを選ばせる単純な形式だけでなく、〈will be ＋ ~ing〉や〈has been ＋過去分詞〉のように、時制と絡めて〈進行形〉か〈受動態〉を選ばせる問題もよく出題されています。主語が「する側」で、空所で問われている他動詞の直後に名詞がある場合は〈進行形〉が正解となり、主語が「される側」で、他動詞なのに空所直後に名詞が見当たらない場合は〈受動態〉が正解となります。

Q 文を完成させるのに、正しい語句を選びましょう。

1. A meeting agenda is usually (preparing / prepared) by one of my subordinates.

2. The effects of our marketing strategy will (discuss / be discussed) at an upcoming meeting.

3. Shinji has (been disappointed / disappointed) since his project idea was rejected.

Point 人物関係と話題の流れをつかもう

チャット形式の文書では、複数の人物が業務の進行状況を確認したり、指示を出し合ったりします。それぞれのコメントは比較的短く、会話調であるため、話の展開が早くなりがちで、発言の意図を問う問題 (例：「○時○分に、" ～ "という発言で、△△さんは何を意図していますか」) が必ず出題されます。詳細の把握よりも人物の関係性や大まかな話の流れをつかむことを目指しましょう。

Q 文書を読んで、設問の答えを(A)と(B)から選びましょう。

Questions 1-2 refer to the following text-message chain.

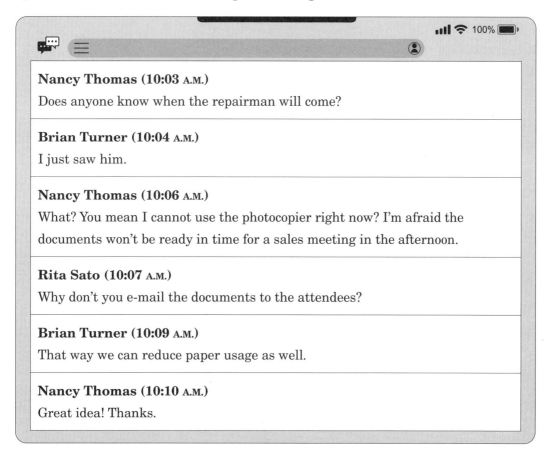

1. What is the problem?

   (A) A copy machine is broken.　　(B) A meeting is late.

2. At 10:10 A.M., what does Ms. Thomas most likely mean when she writes, "Great idea"?

   (A) She received good advice on creating documents.

   (B) She received another way of distributing documents.

Reading Try Out

Select the best answer to complete the sentence.

1. All office supply stocks must ------- in the cabinet in the storage room, and Aron will check them periodically.
(A) keep   (B) keeps   (C) be keeping   (D) be kept

2. Some of my colleagues are ------- in using Instabook to improve our advertising strategies.
(A) interest   (B) to interest   (C) interested   (D) interesting

3. Survey results ------- to our sales representatives yet.
(A) aren't distributing   (C) haven't been distributed
(B) are distributed   (D) have distributed

4. I was asked to load paper into the ------- by Cyrus.
(A) coworker   (B) inspector   (C) photocopier   (D) supervisor

5. The submission ------- for our proposals was extended by a week because of our project leader's hospitalization.
(A) decline   (B) guideline   (C) outline   (D) deadline

Questions 1-3 refer to the following online chat discussion.

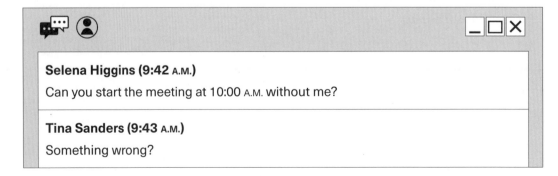

Selena Higgins (9:42 A.M.)
Can you start the meeting at 10:00 A.M. without me?

Tina Sanders (9:43 A.M.)
Something wrong?

Selena Higgins (9:44 A.M.)

I'm stuck in traffic. Can't move.

Tina Sanders (9:49 A.M.)

The client just called. He is coming late, too. He wants us to start at 1:00 P.M. instead.

Selena Higgins (9:50 A.M.)

Great! How about you both?

Tina Sanders (9:52 A.M.)

It's fine, but we may have to rebook the meeting room.

Aaron Eggar (9:55 A.M.)

That's fine with me. My meeting with another client was pushed back to next week. I'll check the vacancy and let you know ASAP.

1. What happened to Ms. Higgins?
   (A) She cannot find the meeting venue.
   (B) She does not feel well.
   (C) She took a wrong bus to work.
   (D) She cannot arrive in time for the morning meeting.

2. At 9:52 A.M., what does Ms. Sanders most likely mean when she writes, "It's fine"?
   (A) She feels good today.
   (B) She can accommodate the new schedule.
   (C) She is happy to meet another client.
   (D) She has already eaten enough.

3. What will Mr. Eggar do next?
   (A) Contact his client
   (B) Start reading a book
   (C) Check on the availability of the room
   (D) Check a bus timetable

Business

接続詞

このユニットでは、企業合併や事業展開などのビジネスに関する英語表現を学びながら、TOEIC®
L&RのPart 1・Part 3・Part 5・Part 6の出題形式を学習します。

Key Words & Phrases

A 音声を聞いて、1〜20の語句とその意味を確認しましょう。その後、ペアで問題を出し合いましょう。

🎧 DL 059　💿 CD2-40

1. negotiation	交渉	☐☐	11. competitor	競合他社	☐☐
2. trade fair	見本市	☐☐	12. merger	合併	☐☐
3. deal	取引	☐☐	13. branch	支社、支店	☐☐
4. make a profit	利益を出す	☐☐	14. launch into ~	～に進出する	☐☐
5. current	現在の	☐☐	15. attorney	弁護士	☐☐
6. performance	業績	☐☐	16. head office	本社	☐☐
7. compromise	妥協する	☐☐	headquarters		☐☐
8. expand	～を拡大する	☐☐	17. relocate	～を移転させる	☐☐
9. recession	不景気	☐☐	18. quarter	四半期	☐☐
depression		☐☐	19. go bankrupt	倒産する	☐☐
10. succeed	～の跡を継ぐ	☐☐	20. in operation	運営［操業］中で	☐☐

B 音声を聞いて、語を書き入れましょう。

🎧 DL 060　💿 CD2-41 ～ 💿 CD2-43

1. The government officially denied that the (① 　　　　　　　) economy is in a
　(② 　　　　　　　).

2. Beniston Industries announced that it has reached an agreement on a
　(① 　　　　　　　) with its (② 　　　　　　　), M&R Technology.

3. KN Foods plans to set up a (① 　　　　　　　) either in Vietnam or Indonesia to
　(② 　　　　　　　) sales channels in Southeast Asia.

Listening Build Up

Part 1	🎧 DL 061 ⦿ CD2-44 ～ ⦿ CD2-47

> **Point** **複数人物の写真は全体を見よう**

複数人物が写っている写真問題の約60%は、音声で読まれる4つの選択肢のうち2つの主語が同じ形で出題されます。本ユニットでは複数人物が写っている写真で、選択肢の主語が2つ同じ形の問題を練習します。読まれた主語に素早く反応できるよう、写真全体を見渡すようにしましょう。

Q 音声を聞いて空所を埋めた後、写真に合う説明文を(A)～(D)から選びましょう。

(A) One of the (　　　　　　) is
　　(　　　　　　　　) coffee from a cup.
(B) One of the women is (　　　　　)
　　(　　　　) at documents.
(C) Some people are (　　　　　　) around
　　a (　　　　).
(D) Some people are (　　　　　　)
　　(　　　　).

Part 3	🎧 DL 062, 063 ⦿ CD2-48 ～ ⦿ CD2-50

> **Point** **意図を問う問題は先読みで発言者を確認しよう**

What does the man [woman / speaker] mean [imply] when he / she says, "～"? や、Why does the man [woman / speaker] say, "～"? の形で聞かれる発言の意図を問う問題は、Part 3 で2問、Part 4で3問出題されます。Part 3では、先読みの際に、女性・男性どちらの発言なのかを確認しておきましょう。話の流れに付いて行き、文脈が理解できれば、それほど難しい問題ではありません。

Q 会話文を聞いて空所を埋めた後、設問の答えを(A)と(B)から選びましょう。

Questions 1 and 2 refer to the following conversation.

W: How's the (1.　　　　　　　　) with Pattana Foods going?

M: Everything's fine. We'll not only get them to sell our products but also
(2.　　　　　　) our new food (3.　　　　　　　) factory. How was the
trade fair?

W: (4.　　　　　) companies approached us. Even if the negotiations with Pattana
Foods fail, we could negotiate with one of them.

M: I'm relieved to hear that.

W: Well, I hope you'll (5.　　　　　　) the deal with Pattana Foods.

M: Thanks. After all, that's my primary goal.

1. What type of business do the speakers probably work for?

   (A) A food manufacturer

   (B) A construction firm

2. What does the man mean when he says, "I'm relieved to hear that"?

   (A) A new project has launched.

   (B) An alternative has been proposed.

Listening Try Out

Select the one statement that best describes what you see in the picture.

(A) (B) (C) (D)

Listen to the conversation and select the best response to each question.

1. Where most likely are the speakers?

(A) At an assembly plant

(B) At a convention center

(C) At an art gallery

(D) At a botanical garden

2. What business does the man work for?

(A) Manufacturing

(B) Landscaping

(C) Consulting

(D) Education

3. What does the woman imply when she says, "We are in a similar situation"?

(A) Her company is making a profit.

(B) Her colleagues need a consultation.

(C) Her customers made the situation worse.

(D) Her department is reducing the budget.

Reading Build Up

接続詞  Grammar Check

→ 空所に適切な日本語を書き入れましょう。

接続詞は、語と語、句と句、(1. 　　　と　　　) をつなぐ役割を果たします。語、句、節を並置して対等の関係でつなぐ、and、but、or などの接続詞を (2. 　　　) 接続詞と呼びます。一方、名詞節や副詞節を導いて、節と節を (3. 　　　) 節と従属節の関係でつなぐ、that、when、because などの接続詞を従属接続詞（従位接続詞）と呼びます。

however「(4. 　　　　　　)」、nevertheless「(5. 　　　　　　　　)」、therefore「(6. 　　　　　　)」などの接続副詞は接続詞的な意味を持っていますが、品詞としては (7. 　　) 詞なので、接続詞のようにコンマで節と節をつなぐことができません。ピリオドやセミコロン (;) で一度文を区切るか、別に接続詞を追加する必要があります。

Part 5

Point　接続詞・前置詞・接続副詞の違いを確認しよう①

TOEIC® L&R では接続詞の意味を問う問題だけでなく、接続詞・前置詞・接続副詞の違いを問う問題が出題されます。コンマで区切られた節が2つある場合は接続詞が、セミコロンで区切られた節が2つある場合は接続副詞が必要です。

Q 文を完成させるのに、正しい語句を選びましょう。

1. Even (if / in case of) negotiations break down, we shouldn't compromise easily.

2. Hermes Travel was determined to expand their business (in spite of / though) it was affected by the global recession.

3. The automaker announced that they will build new plants in both Malaysia (and / or) Thailand.

Point 接続詞と接続副詞を区別しておこう

「接続副詞」は文頭、文中、文末とさまざまな位置に入れることができますが、コンマで独立させて使うのが一般的です。接続詞 although と接続副詞 however、接続詞 while と接続副詞 meanwhile など意味が似ているものは、品詞の違いを意識しながらまとめて確認しておきましょう。

Q 文書を完成させるのに、正しい語や文を選びましょう。

Questions 1-3 refer to the following article.

Cheney's Furniture will extend its business to cleaning services. The president Mike Cheney succeeded his father five years ago. 1. (Over the years Mike honed his skill to restore furniture / The store closed its doors last year). 2. (Then / When) he began working, he noticed stains and scratches in the house to which he delivered furniture, and he voluntarily removed them. "Customers thanked me for my work. We should try what competitors cannot do. 3. (Therefore / However), we are adding room cleaning to our services."

Reading Try Out

  CheckLink

Select the best answer to complete the sentence.

1. RC Petro Corp. and Nexxon Energy Inc. refrained from making any comments ------- they had completed the merger.
   (A) by   (B) pending   (C) till   (D) to

2. ------- business performance of the branch in Mexico is worsening, Mr. Gomez is supposed to visit it.
   (A) Accordingly   (B) Because of   (C) Since   (D) Therefore

3. As to launching into a new field, you should consult not only with your business consultant ------- also your attorney.
   (A) and   (B) but   (C) nor   (D) or

4. Our head office will be ------- to a new building in downtown Atlanta this summer.
   (A) regulated   (B) related   (C) relocated   (D) renovated

5. In the third -------, HealthCare Chemicals increased sales by 27%, supported by growth in sales of their new generic medicine.
   (A) decade   (B) half   (C) quarter   (D) twice

Part 6 CheckLink

Questions 1-4 refer to the following article.

(1 March) Colin Shipyard, whose parent company ------- bankrupt 25 years ago,
1.
will be demolished next month. The real estate developer Willy Realty Group
purchased the site to construct a shopping mall. The ------- will begin in August,
2.
and the stores and restaurants will open in autumn next year. This project will
create over 300 jobs.

At its peak, 20 vessels were inspected at the same time. The shipbuilders of Colin Shipyard specialized in small vessels such as yachts and private cabin cruisers. -------, quite a few boat enthusiasts visited it to take a look at several ships when

3.

Colin Shipyard was in operation.

-------. Besides, the vacant property has been a landmark of the city. The committee

4.

submitted signatures from the residents to save parts of the historically significant architectural structures to the mayor.

1. (A) go
   (B) goes
   (C) went
   (D) to go

2. (A) construct
   (B) constructor
   (C) construction
   (D) constructing

3. (A) Nevertheless
   (B) Otherwise
   (C) Because
   (D) Thus

4. (A) Some of the brick buildings seem to have historical value.
   (B) The company was awarded the best employer prize.
   (C) They can learn how to steer vessels every Sunday.
   (D) The 8th annual boat race will take place next week.

Unit 10

Announcements & Advertisements

このユニットでは、告知や広告に関する英語表現を学びながら、TOEIC® L&RのPart 2・Part 4・Part 5・Part 7の出題形式を学習します。

Key Words & Phrases

A 音声を聞いて、1～20の語句とその意味を確認しましょう。その後、ペアで問題を出し合いましょう。

DL 067　CD2-54

1. advertisement	宣伝、広告	□ □
2. advertise	～を宣伝する	□ □
3. release	発売	□ □
4. flier, flyer	チラシ	□ □
leaflet		□ □
5. impressive	印象的な	□ □
6. eye-catching	目を引く	□ □
7. ad agency	広告代理店	□ □
8. brochure	パンフレット	□ □
9. ideal	理想的な	□ □
10. stunning	大変見事な	□ □
11. post	～を投稿する	□ □

12. social media	SNS	□ □
13. effect	影響	□ □
influence		□ □
14. spokesperson	広報担当者	□ □
15. effective	効果的な	□ □
16. issue	～号	□ □
17. feature	～を特集する、～を目玉にする	
		□ □
18. pay attention to ~	～に注目する	□ □
19. voucher	割引券	□ □
20. present	～を提示する	□ □

B 音声を聞いて、語を書き入れましょう。

DL 068　CD2-55 ～ CD2-57

1. The ad (①　　　　　　　　) sent us the (②　　　　　　　　　　) TV commercial long before the deadline.

2. The (①　　　　　　　　　　　　) for Ristorante Primavera distributed 500 reopening (②　　　　　　　　) with the other staff.

3. The (①　　　　　　　) of (②　　　　　　　) media on youngsters has been so powerful that we can no longer ignore it.

Listening Build Up

Part 2

Point: Yes・No で答えない応答文もある

Part 2の各設問の最初に流れる質問または発言が、Yes / No疑問文になっているものと付加疑問文になっているものを合わせると、全体の約20%を占めます。どちらもYesかNoで返答できますが、実際には、単純にYesかNoで返答していない選択肢が正答になっている問題も頻繁に出題されています。

Q 音声を聞いて空所を埋めた後、適切な応答文を(A)〜(C)から選びましょう。

1. Have you finished revising the (   ) draft?
   (A) Well, not quite (   ).
   (B) Yes, I'm (   ) on Saturday.
   (C) No, our sales weren't (   ).

2. Harry Smith (   ) his new song's release on his Web site, didn't he?
   (A) Yes, he received a (   ) to design a Web site.
   (B) Did (   )? I didn't know that.
   (C) I prefer to (   ) CDs rather than pay for a subscription.

Part 4

DL 070, 071
CD2-60 ~ CD2-62

Point: 言い換えのパターン①　同義語や抽象的な表現への言い換え

「言い換え」は TOEIC® L&R でよく用いられます。例えば、音声に出た coworker が選択肢では同義語の colleague に、音声に出た troubles with the engine が、選択肢では抽象的な technical difficulties に言い換えられます。同義語や似たような表現は意識してまとめて覚えましょう。

Q 説明文を聞いて空所を埋めた後、設問の答えを(A)と(B)から選びましょう。

Questions 1 and 2 refer to the following (1.   ).

W: Are you looking for delicious and aromatic tea that arrives in a timely manner? Rou Tea House has a (2.   ) service for tea lovers. A selection of tea is (3.   ) to your mailbox every week. Let's make tea drinking part of your daily (4.   ). If you access our Web site and (5.   ) for our service today, we will offer you free samples of tea bags!

1. What is being advertised?
   (A) A beverage   (B) An online class

2. What does the speaker offer?
   (A) Some product samples   (B) An information package

Listening Try Out

Part 2

Listen to the question or statement and the three responses. Then select the best response to the question or statement.

1. (A) (B) (C)

2. (A) (B) (C)

3. (A) (B) (C)

Part 4

Listen to the talk and select the best response to each question.

1. What event will be held this weekend?
(A) A local meeting
(B) An artist fair
(C) A recording
(D) A food exhibition

2. Who is Andy Mason?
(A) A mayor
(B) A curator
(C) An organizer
(D) A café owner

3. What does the speaker imply when he says, "hurry to enjoy their signature coffee"?
(A) The number of offerings is limited.
(B) An item can be discounted.
(C) A shop will go bankrupt.
(D) The shop does not have enough seats.

Reading Build Up

→空所に適切な日本語や英語を書き入れましょう。

前置詞は、名詞・代名詞・(1.　　　　　) 詞などの前に置かれて、主に場所・位置や時を表す品詞で、日本語の「〜に」「〜へ」「〜の」といった助詞に近い働きをします。

He put the flyer on the table. の on the table の部分は、「テーブル (2.　　　　　)」という意味で、動詞 put を修飾する (3.　　　) 詞句の働きをしています。一方、He read the flyer on the table. の on the table の部分は「テーブル (4.　　　　　)」というように、直前の名詞句 the flyer を修飾する形容詞句の働きをしています。

before「〜の前」、(5.　　　　　)「〜の後」、since「〜以来」、(6.　　　　　)「〜までずっと」など、意味も同じままで接続詞としても前置詞としても用いられる語もあります。一方で、例えば、接続詞としては「というのは〜だから」の意味を持ち、前置詞としては「〜のために」や「〜にとって」の意味を持つ for や、接続詞としては「〜なので」や「〜時」の意味を持ち、前置詞としては「〜として」の意味を持つ (7.　　　) のように、接続詞として使われる場合と前置詞として使われる場合で、意味が異なる語もあります。

Part 5

Point 接続詞・前置詞・接続副詞の違いを確認しよう②

TOEIC® L&R では前置詞の意味を問う問題だけでなく、前置詞・接続詞・接続副詞の違いを問う問題が出題されます。前置詞の後ろは名詞・代名詞・動名詞という名詞系列の語（句）が来ますので、空所の後ろの形をしっかり確認しましょう。

Q 文を完成させるのに、正しい語句を選びましょう。

1. Esperanza Catering has been busy preparing for its reopening (from / since) its announcement in the local newspaper last month.

2. They succeeded in making an eye-catching video ad (by / near) having detailed meetings with the ad agency many times.

3. Grandma's Pastries ordered the printing of two-color leaflets instead of full-color brochures (because / due to) budget restrictions.

形式が分からない文書は、最初に導入部をチェックする

ウェブサイト、メール、オンラインチャットなど一目で形式が分かる文書以外は、枠外にある導入部を最初にチェックするようにしましょう。そこには advertisement「広告」、article「記事」、notice「通知」、press release「報道発表」など、これから読む文書の形式が一言で示されているため、最初に目を通しておくと内容を理解しやすくなります。

Q 文書を読んで、設問の答えを(A)と(B)から選びましょう。

Questions 1-2 refer to the following advertisement.

House for sale $425,000

181 South Park
(Property #122)

This two-story brick home is ready to move straight into. It's ideal for a young family, with two schools within a 10-minute walk.

The first floor has an entrance hallway with a bathroom and a large living room. The ultra-modern kitchen is perfect for cooking delicious meals.

The second floor has a master bedroom with its own private bathroom. There are two more bedrooms with an additional bathroom.

Contact us at 099-222-78986. Daniela Morris, one of our experienced staff members, will show you around the house.

Alexandria Residential Co.

1. What is suggested about property #122?
   (A) It is located within walking distance of educational institutions.
   (B) It is a traditional mansion with classical furniture.

2. Who most likely is Daniela Morris?
   (A) A landlord
   (B) A sales representative

Reading   Try Out

Part 5

Select the best answer to complete the sentence.

1. After the stunning advertisement in which the cosmetic company uses an unknown new actress, the lipstick became a big hit ------- young women.
(A) among   (B) during   (C) for   (D) while

2. One of our staff carelessly posted information about our secret sales on social media without ------- of its effect.
(A) to think   (B) to thinking   (C) thinking   (D) thoughtful

3. ------- the spokesperson, Eichen Furnishing is opening up a new branch in Glendale.
(A) According to   (B) Contrary to   (C) Owing to   (D) Thanks to

4. It's essential for many companies to make their social media ads ------- because about 30% of Internet users today search for new products after seeing them.
(A) abstract   (B) effective   (C) fragile   (D) obscure

5. All the staff are excited to hear that a fashion magazine will ------- their new line of bags in the autumn issue.
(A) frighten   (B) facilitate   (C) feature   (D) fertilize

Part 7

Questions **1-4** refer to the following Web page.

https://www.mandel_consulting.com/news/new_courses

Mandel Consulting Group to Start New Training Courses

These days business trends are changing very rapidly, and it isn't unusual to see a great change take place in a short period of time. All industries are getting more and more competitive. —[1]—. In such situations more companies pay attention to leadership, which will enable them to achieve further development. —[2]—. So, in response to their needs, Mandel Consulting Group has put together a wide range of courses to help you become a real leader.

We have four courses available: a 5-week intensive course, a 3-month course, a 6-month course, as well as a 15-week online course. —[3]—. At first you will learn the definition of leadership, its styles, and the required skills. Then you will get hands-on practice by discussing and role-playing actual cases.

In celebration of the start of Mandel Consulting Group's new training courses, you can receive a 5% discount on course fees. After watching a video about our courses, a voucher will be made available to you. —[4]—. Save the voucher and show it to us when registering. The link to the video is: https://www.mandel_consulting.com/course/guide_014325.html

If you have any questions, send us an e-mail at nextleader@mandel_consulting.com or call us at 930-571-9225 during regular business hours.

1. What is indicated about the courses?

(A) They will provide job opportunities.

(B) Some of them are highly competitive.

(C) They will be newly offered.

(D) All of them will be held online.

2. What is NOT included in their course contents?

(A) What practice is effective for leadership

(B) What types of leadership there are

(C) What leadership is all about

(D) What skills are necessary for leadership

3. How can some customers receive a discount?

(A) By sending an e-mail

(B) By presenting a coupon

(C) By responding to a customer survey

(D) By taking a trial lesson

4. In which of the positions marked [1], [2], [3], and [4] does the following sentence best belong?

"All courses will start on September 5th."

(A) [1]   (B) [2]   (C) [3]   (D) [4]

Unit 11

Personnel

このユニットでは、昇進・異動・退職などの人事に関する英語表現を学びながら、TOEIC® L&Rの
Part 1・Part 3・Part 5・Part 6の出題形式を学習します。

Key Words & Phrases

A 音声を聞いて、1〜20の語句とその意味を確認しましょう。その後、ペアで問題を出し合
いましょう。

🎧 DL 075　💿 CD3-02

1. assign	～を任命する	☐ ☐	11. subsidiary	子会社	☐ ☐
appoint		☐ ☐	12. suitable	適切な	☐ ☐
2. accumulate experience	経験を積む		13. take over ~	～を引き継ぐ	☐ ☐
		☐ ☐	14. hire	～を雇う	☐ ☐
3. division	部門	☐ ☐	employ		☐ ☐
department		☐ ☐	15. resign	辞任する	☐ ☐
4. application	申請書	☐ ☐	16. replace	～の後任になる	☐ ☐
5. promotion	昇進	☐ ☐	17. retire	(定年)退職する	☐ ☐
6. supervisor	上司、管理者	☐ ☐	18. in-house	社内の	☐ ☐
7. evaluation	評価	☐ ☐	19. be responsible for ~		☐ ☐
8. be eligible for ~	～の資格がある	☐ ☐	be in charge of ~	～を担当している	
9. transfer	～を異動させる	☐ ☐			☐ ☐
10. senior manager	上級管理者	☐ ☐	20. benefits (package)	福利厚生	☐ ☐

B 音声を聞いて、語を書き入れましょう。

🎧 DL 076　💿 CD3-03 ～ 💿 CD3-05

1. The man introduced himself to my (① 　　　　　　　　　　) as a new sales rep
(② 　　　　　　　　　　) for our company.

2. Billy got (① 　　　　　　　　　　) to our (② 　　　　　　　　　　) in Singapore.

3. Ms. Stride will (① 　　　　　　) soon, and I was (② 　　　　　　　　　　) to take
over the project from her.

Listening　Build Up

Part 1　　　　　DL 077　　CD3-06 ～ CD3-09

Point 写真に写っているものは全て登場するつもりで聞こう

複数人物が写っている写真問題の約 20% が、音声で読まれる選択肢の主語が全て異なる形で出題されます。本ユニットでは複数人物が写っている写真で、選択肢の主語が全て異なる形の問題を練習します。写真内に登場する人物と物は全て主語になる可能性がありますが、人物と動作（時制と態）、物と人物の位置関係を正確に聞き取り、正答を選べるようになりましょう。

Q 音声を聞いて空所を埋めた後、写真に合う説明文を (A) ～ (D) から選びましょう。

(A) Some (　　　　　　) are being (　　　　　　　　)
　　from the shelf.
(B) Some (　　　　　　　　　　) have been
　　(　　　　　　　　　　) on the floor.
(C) The (　　　　　　) are (　　　　　　)
　　each other.
(D) The (　　　　　　　　) is (　　　　　　　　)
　　the room.

Part 3　　　　　DL 078, 079　　CD3-10 ～ CD3-12

Point 言い換えのパターン② 品詞の変換による言い換え

「言い換え」は TOEIC® L&R でよく用いられます。音声では evaluate a performance「業績を評価する」が流れて、選択肢では a performance evaluation「業績評価」が用いられるというように、音声で使われた表現が語順や品詞を変えて選択肢に登場するということがよくあります。

Q 会話文を聞いて空所を埋めた後、設問の答えを (A) と (B) から選びましょう。

Questions 1 and 2 refer to the following conversation with three speakers.

M1: OK, everyone, this is our (1.　　　　　　　　) section. Silvain, the lab leader here, will
answer your questions.

M2: Welcome to Coughlin Pharmaceuticals' most advanced (2.　　　　　　　　　　　).

W: Hi, Silvain. How long does it take a new (3.　　　　　　　), like me, to get
assigned to this lab?

M2: Well, it took me almost five years. I needed to accumulate experience in some
other (4.　　　　　　　　).

1. What does Silvain do?
   (A) He guides a tour.
   (B) He leads the lab.

2. What is required in order for the woman to work in the lab?
   (A) Active participation in some different projects
   (B) Accumulating experience in various departments

Listening Try Out

Part 1

Select the one statement that best describes what you see in the picture.

(A) (B) (C) (D)

Part 3

Listen to the conversation and select the best response to each question.

1. What task does the man say he finished?
  (A) Careful reading of material
  (B) An arrangement for a meeting
  (C) A training for new employees
  (D) A handover of his duties

2. What are the speakers mainly discussing?
  (A) Job applications
  (B) Office relocation
  (C) Package tours
  (D) Employee promotion

3. What does the woman imply when she says, "I know what you mean"?
  (A) She agrees that there are no potential applicants.
  (B) She understands how fair the supervisors' evaluations are.
  (C) She notices that many applicants are eligible for promotion.
  (D) She recognizes whose opinions will be plausible.

Reading Build Up

代名詞

Grammar Check

→空所に適切な日本語や英語を書き入れましょう。

人称代名詞は人称・格・数によって変化します。人称には、「私」などの「話し手」を指す (1.　　　) 人称、「あなた」などの「聞き手」を指す (2.　　) 人称、それ以外の第三者や物を指す (3.　　　) 人称があります。格には主語として用いられる (4.　　　) 格、後ろに名詞を伴って所有を表す (5.　　　　) 格、動詞や前置詞の目的語として用いられる (6.　　　) 格があります。数にはI「私は」とwe「私たちは」のように、単数と複数があります。さらに人称代名詞には、「～のもの」を意味する所有代名詞と「～自身」を意味する再帰代名詞も含まれます。

指示代名詞は、this「これ」、these「これら」、that「あれ」、(7.　　　　　)「あれら」など目の前にあるものを指したり、文中で前後に述べた語句の内容を指したりします。

不定代名詞は、one、some、any、both、all、anyone、somebody、nothingなど、不特定の人や物を指します。

Part 5

Point 人称代名詞を再確認しよう

Part 5では、代名詞の問題が毎回約2問出題されています。anyoneなどの不定代名詞が問われることもありますが、ほとんどが人称代名詞の問題なので、人称・格・数をしっかり確認しておきましょう。

Q 文を完成させるのに、正しい語を選びましょう。

1. Vanessa will be transferred to the sales department where (she / her) has long wanted to work.

2. Atlantic Trading Company appointed Mr. Stanton as senior manager to (it / its) overseas subsidiary.

3. Mr. Radcliff applied (him / himself) to his work in order to give himself a chance at a promotion.

Point 代名詞が指すものを考えながら読もう

Part 6で出題される代名詞の問題には、Part 5と同様に単独の文の中で解ける問題と、前の文中にある情報を基に正解を選ばなければならない問題があります。後者のタイプでは、代名詞が指しているものが、単数なのか複数なのか、人物なのか物なのかなどをよく見て解答を選びましょう。

Q 文書を完成させるのに、正しい語や文を選びましょう。

Questions 1-3 refer to the following notice.

Liz Lee will join 1.(us / our) design group next Monday. Liz earned the Best Creative Toy Design Award last year. Moreover, Fun Toy Co., where Liz just worked as a team leader, has increased its sales over the past four years. 2.(This / These) shows that her leadership ability is exceptional. To welcome her as our new manager, a lunch party will be held at the cafeteria at noon on Friday. 3.(Come and meet her there / Please let me know what time is convenient for you).

Reading Try Out

Part 5

Select the best answer to complete the sentence.

1. Today AN Network announced that ------- elected Mr. Lu as CEO.

  (A) they   (B) their   (C) them   (D) themselves

2. Our supervisor recommended Mike as a team leader after evaluating -------
performance.

  (A) he   (B) his   (C) him   (D) himself

3. If you know ------- suitable to take over the project from Ms. Rodriguez, please let me
know by e-mail.

  (A) something   (B) it   (C) anyone   (D) both

4. We need to hire a new worker to ------- Shannon, who is resigning next month.

  (A) replace   (B) introduce   (C) pay   (D) locate

5. I am so sad to know that Mr. Raymond is going to ------- at the end of this month.

  (A) remodel   (B) remark   (C) repair   (D) retire

Part 6
CheckLink

Questions 1-4 refer to the following e-mail.

To: All staff <staff@ryansclothing.uk>

From: Park Mao <parkmao@ryansclothing.uk>

Date: 15 March

Subject: Job Posting

This is the information on the in-house job opening. ------- have an opening
1.
for Store Manager in the Edinburgh branch, which will open in December. The
successful applicant will be responsible for management of staff, stock control,
budget adjustment, and analysis for achieving sales targets. In addition, he/she

should have mentorship to support the staff physically and ------. A company
2.
residence and car are provided for free. ------.
3.

To apply for this position, 15 years of experience working for our company is
required. It is ------ that he/she was assigned to at least two departments. If
4.
you are interested in the position, reply to this e-mail by the end of this week.
Applicants selected will be contacted to schedule an interview after 1 April.

1. (A) It
   (B) You
   (C) We
   (D) Theirs

2. (A) automatically
   (B) occasionally
   (C) potentially
   (D) mentally

3. (A) A retirement farewell party will have been prepared in a few days.
   (B) A gym membership in the fitness center near the office is also available.
   (C) They should decide to take advantage of our benefits package in advance.
   (D) It will take 50 minutes to drive to the commercial facility.

4. (A) prefer
   (B) preference
   (C) preferable
   (D) preferably

Unit 12

Health & Environment

このユニットでは、健康や環境に関する英語表現を学びながら、TOEIC® L&R の Part 2・Part 4・Part 5・Part 7 の出題形式を学習します。

Key Words & Phrases

A 音声を聞いて、1〜20の語句とその意味を確認しましょう。その後、ペアで問題を出し合いましょう。

DL 083　CD3-16

1. make an appointment	予約する ☐☐	**11.** insurance	保険 ☐☐
2. prescription	処方箋 ☐☐	**12.** sustainable	持続可能な ☐☐
3. pharmacy	薬局 ☐☐	**13.** infectious	伝染性の ☐☐
4. garbage	ごみ ☐☐	**14.** disease	病気 ☐☐
trash	☐☐	illness	☐☐
5. disposal	処理 ☐☐	**15.** prevent	〜を予防する ☐☐
6. collect	〜を回収する ☐☐	**16.** symptom	症状 ☐☐
7. pollution	汚染 ☐☐	**17.** consultation	相談 ☐☐
8. medical checkup	健康診断 ☐☐	**18.** patient	患者 ☐☐
9. clean(-)up	清掃 ☐☐	**19.** reception	受付 ☐☐
10. sort	〜を分類する ☐☐	**20.** follow *one's* advice	〜の助言に従う ☐☐

B 音声を聞いて、語を書き入れましょう。

DL 084　CD3-17 ～ CD3-19

1. Ms. Selvidge called Heart Clinic to make an (①   ) for an annual (②   ) checkup.

2. This handbook teaches us how to (①   ) (②   ) in this area.

3. The (①   ) (②   ) Dr. Hudson's advice on how to lose weight by eating fruits and vegetables.

Listening Build Up

Part 2

🎧 DL 085 · CD3-20 · CD3-21

Point 否定疑問文と選択疑問文の応答の仕方に注意

否定疑問文とは、"Aren't you ~?" や "Didn't you ~?" などの否定形で始まり、「〜ではないのですか」という意味になる疑問文です。否定疑問文への応答は、Yes の後ろには肯定文が、No の後ろには否定文が続きます。選択疑問文とは、or をつなぎにして列挙された2つ以上のものや動作の中から、どれかを選択させようとする疑問文で、Yes や No では返答できません。

Q 音声を聞いて空所を埋めた後、適切な応答文を (A) 〜 (C) から選びましょう。

1. Didn't you make an (　　　　　　　　　)?

(A) Yes, (　　　) do.

(B) Yes, I called the (　　　　　) three days ago.

(C) No, I don't have any time to (　　　　　　).

2. Is this prescription or over-the-counter (　　　　　　)?

(A) You can buy it at any (　　　　　　　　) without a prescription.

(B) (　　　　　) this one with a lot of water.

(C) Yes, we (　　　　　) a lot over the counter.

Part 4

🎧 DL 086, 087 · CD3-22 ~ CD3-24

Point 図表問題の「先読み」と心の準備①

図表問題は「先読み」の段階で、図表と選択肢の両方を確認します。例えば、次のように図表に品目と価格の一覧が記載されており、選択肢に品目が並んでいる表タイプの図表問題の場合、音声では品目には触れられず、価格についてのみ言及されます。つまり、表タイプの問題では、「選択肢で触れられていない方」について言及されるということを覚えておきましょう。

medicine	price
Aspirin	$4.20
Ibuprofen EX	$9.50
Naproxen Generic	$13
Acetaminophen A	$18

選択肢
(A) Aspirin
(B) Ibuprofen EX
(C) Naproxen Generic
(D) Acetaminophen A

音声
🔊

Q 説明文を聞いて空所を埋めた後、設問の答えを(A)と(B)から選びましょう。

Questions 1 and 2 refer to the following (1.   ) message and schedule.

Shift Schedule for September	
Time	Dentist
9:00 A.M. – Noon	Sala Evans
1:00 P.M. – 4:00 P.M.	Peter Williams

M: Hi, Mr. Lee. I'm calling from Pine Hill Dental Clinic. We have your
(2.   ) for September fifth. Unfortunately, your attending
dentist Mike Dixon will not be (3.   ) in September, so Peter
Williams will fill in for him. But if you want to see Mike, you must
(4.   ) the appointment and book on another day. Please call us back
about your (5.   ).

1. Where does the speaker work?
(A) At a dental clinic
(B) At a pharmacy

2. Look at the graphic. In which time slot has a change been made?
(A) 9:00 A.M. – Noon
(B) 1:00 P.M. – 4:00 P.M.

Listening Try Out

Part 2

Listen to the question or statement and the three responses. Then select the best response to the question or statement.

1. (A) (B) (C)

2. (A) (B) (C)

3. (A) (B) (C)

Part 4

Listen to the talk while looking at the graphic and select the best response to each question.

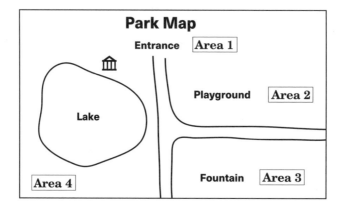

1. Why does the speaker thank the listeners?

   (A) They have participated in an event.

   (B) They will mark an anniversary.

   (C) They completed a project.

   (D) They got an award.

2. Look at the graphic. Which area will the listeners work in?

   (A) Area 1   (C) Area 3

   (B) Area 2   (D) Area 4

3. What will the listeners do next?

   (A) Apply for a job   (C) Meet a park ranger

   (B) Visit a destination   (D) Get some tools

Reading Build Up

不定詞

→空所に適切な日本語や英語を書き入れましょう。

to 不定詞には、①「～すること」の意味で、主語、補語、目的語になり、名詞のような働きをする (1.　　　　) 詞的用法、②「～するための」「～すべき」などの意味で、後ろから名詞を修飾する (2.　　　　) 詞的用法、③「～する (3.　　　　　　)」「～して」「もし～なら」などの意味で、名詞以外の品詞を修飾する副詞的用法があります。

what to read「何を (4.　　　　　　) か」、when to start the project「そのプロジェクトをいつ (5.　　　　　　) か」、whether to join the party「パーティーに (6.　　　　　) かどうか」というように、〈疑問詞 + to 不定詞〉は名詞句を作ります。

〈使役動詞 + 目的語〉の後ろには動詞の原形が来ます。〈let + 目的語 + 動詞の原形〉で「…に～させてあげる」、〈have + 目的語 + 動詞の原形〉で「…に～してもらう」、〈(7.　　　　　) + 目的語 + 動詞の原形〉で「…に(強制的に)～させる」の意味になります。

Part 5

Point) Part 5 で不定詞が正答になることは多くない

Part 5 の語形変化や品詞を問う問題の選択肢に、to 不定詞が並んでいることがよくありますが、実は to 不定詞が正答になることはあまり多くありません。とは言っても、テスト全体で頻繁に出現しますので、しっかり復習しておきましょう。

Q 文を完成させるのに、正しい語句を選びましょう。

1. It is very important (protect / to protect) the natural environment.

2. After joining a gym near her office, she was happy (lose / to lose) five kilograms in two months.

3. I let my children (run / to run) around the park for hours as they pleased.

ダブルパッセージ問題の設問設定

ダブルパッセージの問題には設問が5つありますが、そのうち1〜2問は、複数の文書を参照しなければならないクロスレファレンス問題です。まずは1つの文書を参照して答えられる問題を確実に正解するところから始めましょう。ダブルパッセージの問題は、6分程度での解答を目指しましょう。

Q 2つの文書を読んで、設問の答えを(A)と(B)から選びましょう。

Questions 1-3 refer to the following Web page and e-mail.

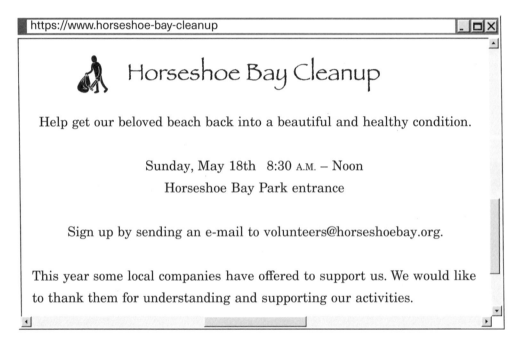

https://www.horseshoe-bay-cleanup

Horseshoe Bay Cleanup

Help get our beloved beach back into a beautiful and healthy condition.

Sunday, May 18th   8:30 A.M. − Noon
Horseshoe Bay Park entrance

Sign up by sending an e-mail to volunteers@horseshoebay.org.

This year some local companies have offered to support us. We would like to thank them for understanding and supporting our activities.

To:	Samuel Murphy <smurphy@webmail.com>
From:	Barry Glansford <volunteers@horseshoebay.org>
Date:	Monday, May 12
Subject:	Preparations for Horseshoe Bay Cleanup

Hello, Mr. Murphy,

A big thank you for volunteering to help out at this year's Horseshoe Bay Cleanup. New people like you are more than welcome.

Please bring sturdy gloves. We will provide the tongs and garbage bags. As refreshments will be donated by Bill's Grocer and Horseshoe Café, you don't need to bring lunch.

See you on Sunday!

Barry Glansford
Horseshoe Bay Cleanup Committee Leader

1. What is the purpose of the Web page?
   (A) To report a problem
   (B) To recruit volunteers

2. What is suggested about Bill's Grocer?
   (A) It is located in Horseshoe Bay.
   (B) It produces cleaning tools.

3. What is suggested about Samuel Murphy?
   (A) He is a new participant.
   (B) He has worked for a cleaning company.

Reading Try Out

Select the best answer to complete the sentence.

1. Shannon doesn't have any insurance ------- dental treatment.
(A) cover (B) to cover (C) covered (D) will cover

2. The employees are very surprised ------- that their company is going to shift to sustainable materials.
(A) know (B) to know (C) knowing (D) knew

3. Atlas Pharmaceuticals had the hospital ------- a clinical trial for its new medicine.
(A) conduct (B) to conduct (C) conducting (D) conducted

4. This Web site tells you in detail how to ------- infectious diseases.
(A) maintain (B) preserve (C) prevent (D) suffer

5. The municipal government tried to make the residents ------- the local rules to separate trash by imposing a fine on violations.
(A) subscribe (B) eliminate (C) protect (D) follow

Questions 1-5 refer to the following notice and e-mail.

Chase Away the January Blues

January, which comes after the excitement of the holiday season, is a time when some people feel under the weather, have no appetite, can't sleep well at night or feel depressed.

Here are four things you can do yourself at home to minimize the effect of the symptoms.

1. Get as much daylight as possible

2. Work up a bit of a sweat

3. Sleep well

4. Meditate for 10 minutes a day

If they don't work, I recommend you consult a specialist as soon as possible. There are occupational health psychologists and physicians at our office. Please e-mail me at counselling@deltatek.com to make an appointment.

Consultation Hours

Day	Time	Counselor
Monday	Noon – 8 P.M.	Dr. Hughes
Wednesday	11 A.M. – 7 P.M.	Dr. Beckmann
Thursday	10 A.M. – 5 P.M.	Dr. Abbot
Friday	Noon – 8 P.M.	Dr. Steiner

Michelle Garfield, HR Section Manager

Delta Tek

To:	Michelle Garfield <counselling@deltatek.com>
From:	Enrique Gonzalez <egonzalez@deltatek.com>
Date:	January 17
Subject:	Counselling Appointment

Ms. Garfield,

I tried all of the tips you wrote, but they didn't work. I have all the symptoms you mentioned in the notice.

When I attended a seminar at the civic center two years ago, I listened to Dr. Steiner's lecture. Her talk was really easy to understand and very helpful. I want to get counselling with her.

Thank you.

Enrique Gonzalez

1. What is the purpose of the notice?

   (A) To promote a medical checkup
   (B) To ask for data about patients
   (C) To announce counselors on standby
   (D) To detail a way of spending a holiday

2. What is suggested about the appointment application?

   (A) It is not accepted by means other than e-mail.
   (B) Its deadline is likely to be extended.
   (C) Its form can be received at the reception desk.
   (D) It must be submitted with a recommendation.

3. In the notice, the word "work" in paragraph 3, line 1, is closest in meaning to

   (A) create
   (B) labor
   (C) function
   (D) study

4. What day will Mr. Gonzales most likely get counselling?

   (A) Monday
   (B) Wednesday
   (C) Thursday
   (D) Friday

5. What is indicated about Mr. Gonzalez?

   (A) He had health problems two years ago.
   (B) He followed Ms. Garfield's advice.
   (C) He held a seminar at the civic center.
   (D) He works as an engineer at Delta Tek.

Unit 13

Finance & Banking

このユニットでは、融資や銀行業務などの金融に関する英語表現を学びながら、TOEIC® L&R の
Part 2・Part 3・Part 5・Part 7 の出題形式を学習します。

Key Words & Phrases

A 音声を聞いて、1～20の語句とその意味を確認しましょう。その後、ペアで問題を出し合いましょう。

⬇ DL 091　◉ CD3-30

1. transaction	取引	☐☐	**11.** accountant	会計士	☐☐
2. transact	(取引など)を行う	☐☐	**12.** debt	借金、負債	☐☐
3. mortgage	住宅ローン	☐☐	**13.** financial	財務の、金融の	☐☐
	housing loan	☐☐	**14.** digit	桁	☐☐
4. expense	出費	☐☐	**15.** stockholder	株主	☐☐
5. calculate	～を計算する	☐☐		shareholder	☐☐
6. interest	利息、利子	☐☐	**16.** withdraw	～を引き出す	☐☐
7. payment	支払い	☐☐	**17.** investor	投資家	☐☐
8. additional	追加の	☐☐	**18.** fiscal year	事業年度	☐☐
	extra	☐☐	**19.** deposit	～を預金する	☐☐
9. fee	手数料	☐☐	**20.** teller	銀行の窓口係	☐☐
10. account	口座	☐☐			

B 音声を聞いて、語を書き入れましょう。

⬇ DL 092　◉ CD3-31 ～ ◉ CD3-33

1. A small change in (①   ) rates can make a big difference in our
(②   ) payment.

2. There is a transaction (①   ) for (②   ) transfers.

3. Mr. Wu must check the (①   ) statements for the annual
(②   ) meeting.

Listening Build Up

Part 2　　　🎧 DL 093　◎ CD3-34　◎ CD3-35

Point 依頼・申し出・許可に対しては決まり文句で解答できることが多い

「～してくれませんか」という〈依頼〉、「～いたしましょうか」という〈申し出〉、「～してもいいですか」という〈許可の要望〉への応答は、パターン化された表現で対応できることが多いので、決まり文句を確認しておきましょう。

Q 音声を聞いて空所を埋めた後、適切な応答文を(A)～(C)から選びましょう。

1. Why don't we attend his seminar on corporate (　　　　　　)?

   (A) I (　　　　　) to say thank you.

   (B) I'd love (　　　).

   (C) I told him to (　　　　) the company.

2. (　　　　　) you show me the (　　　　　　　　　) report?

   (A) Sure, (　　　　) you go.

   (B) The (　　　　　　　　　) is right.

   (C) Down the (　　　　).

Part 3　　　🎧 DL 094, 095　◎ CD3-36 ～ ◎ CD3-38

Point 会話文では短い返答が使われることがある

Could you write your name down here?「こちらに記名してくださいますか」に対して、正式には Should I write here?「ここに書いたらよいですか」や Is here OK?「こちらでよいですか」と返答するところを、特に会話では Here? や Here OK? だけを用いて、断片的に短く返答することがあります。

Q 会話文を聞いて空所を埋めた後、設問の答えを(A)と(B)から選びましょう。

Questions 1 and 2 refer to the following conversation.

W: Mr. Winters, before you sign the (^{1.}　　　　　　　　　) application, there are a few things we have to (^{2.}　　　　　　) to you.

M: OK. Fine.

W: Your monthly expense is calculated based on an (^{3.}　　　　　　　　) rate, which is revised annually. That is to say, your monthly expense will be adjusted accordingly every April. Let me remind you that any delayed (^{4.}　　　　　　　　　) may result in additional fees.

106

1. What are the speakers talking about?

    (A) A housing loan

    (B) Start-up companies

2. What does the woman warn of?

    (A) Monthly payments are completely fixed.

    (B) An extra fee might be charged.

Listening Try Out

Part 2

Listen to the question or statement and the three responses. Then select the best response to the question or statement.

1. (A) (B) (C)

2. (A) (B) (C)

3. (A) (B) (C)

Part 3

Listen to the conversation while looking at the graphic and select the best response to each question.

Brandon Taylor

Office address: 8240 Delton Way, Hennepin, MN
Phone number: 3329-5515
Fax number: 3329-5516
E-mail address: brandon@taylorplanning.com
Business Hours: Monday–Friday, 9 A.M. to 5 P.M.
*Please send inquiries by e-mail outside business hours.

---

1. What is the woman looking at?

(A) An invoice

(B) A price list for gas

(C) A brochure

(D) A university Web site

2. What concern does the woman express?

(A) Getting an invoice reissued might take a long time.

(B) Being in debt could affect her education expenses.

(C) Her garage does not have enough space for two cars.

(D) Her application for a loan will not be approved.

3. Look at the graphic. Which information will the woman use to contact Brandon?

(A) Office address

(B) Phone number

(C) Fax number

(D) E-mail address

Reading Build Up

助動詞

→空所に適切な日本語や英語を書き入れましょう。

助動詞の後ろは動詞の原形になります。主な助動詞は、「～するつもりだ」「～だろう」の意味を持つwill、「～できる」「～する可能性がある」の意味を持つ (1.　　　　　　)、「～してもよい」「～ (2.　　　　　　　　　　)」の意味を持つmay、「～しなければならない」「～に違いない」の意味を持つ (3.　　　　　　)、「～ (4.　　　　　　　　)」「～なはずだ」の意味を持つshouldの5つです。

cannotは「～できない」と「～ (5.　　　　　　　　　)」の意味に、may notは「～してはいけない」という不許可の意味に、must notは「～してはいけない」という強い禁止の意味になります。

助動詞を2つ続けることはできないので、「～できるだろう」という意味を表す場合は、will canやcan willではなく、will be (6.　　　　　　) to *do*を使います。また、「～しなければならないかもしれない」という意味を表す場合も、may mustやmust mayではなく、may (7.　　　　　) to *do*を使います。

Part 5

Point 助動詞の後ろは原形

助動詞に関する問題の出題数は減少傾向にあります。ただ、「助動詞の後ろが原形」ということを問う、基本的な問題は今でも出題されています。

Q 文を完成させるのに、正しい語句を選びましょう。

1. A foreigner cannot (open / opens) a bank account online and needs to visit a bank branch.

2. If you often miss credit card payments, you (can't / mustn't) pass the screening for a mortgage.

3. To avoid a deficit for five consecutive quarters, we definitely (must will / will have to) reduce the overall cost by about 12%.

Part 7

Point 固有名詞・日付が複数の文書をつなぐカギ

Unit 12でも説明したように、ダブルパッセージの5つの設問のうち1〜2問は、複数の文書を参照しなければならないクロスレファレンス問題です。クロスレファレンス問題では、人物名や会社名などの固有名詞、所在地、日付、曜日などの場所と日時について述べている箇所に注目すると、2つの文書のつながりを見つけやすくなります。

Q 2つの文書を読んで、設問の答えを(A)と(B)から選びましょう。

Questions 1-3 refer to the following flyer and letter.

Open Account—Get $200!

First-time Customers Only
March 1 to August 31

Otto Bank offers a special cash bonus program to customers who open a new account. All new members who open an Otto Bank account during the limited promotion period are eligible for this one-time perk.

June 12
Carl Burkes
34 Roxie Road
Chicago, IL 60607

Dear Mr. Burkes,

Thank you for opening a new account with Otto Bank. Your ID and 8-digit passcode for online banking are below.

ID: burkes67639dcx-ottob
Passcode: hdelso9r

We hope we will have a long-term relationship with you and to offer you the best service.

Sincerely Yours,

Otto Bank

1. What is suggested about Otto Bank?
   (A) It runs a promotional campaign regularly.
   (B) It plans to get new customers.

2. What is the purpose of the letter?
   (A) To ask about a new partnership
   (B) To provide some information

3. What is suggested about Mr. Burkes?
   (A) He will get cash.
   (B) He failed to activate his online banking account.

$\mathbf{R}$eading Try Out

Select the best answer to complete the sentence.

1. Our annual general meeting of stockholders this year will ------- solely by means of remote communication.

(A) hold   (B) held   (C) holding   (D) be held

2. As Eastern Trust Bank's ATM service isn't available during the long holiday, we ------- withdraw some money before it.

(A) can't   (B) had   (C) ought   (D) should

3. In late September investors ------- download the PDF file of our financial reports for this fiscal year.

(A) will be   (B) is able to   (C) can be   (D) will be able to

4. A bachelor's degree in accounting or a related field is required to be an ------- or an auditor.

(A) accountant   (B) applicant   (C) immigrant   (D) inhabitant

5. Rosenthal Digital Bank offers higher ------- rates than other major banks.

(A) budget   (B) finance   (C) interest   (D) revenue

Questions 1-5 refer to the following article and e-mail.

Medan (October 5)—Tates, one of the biggest banks in Indonesia, suffered a system failure that disrupted its ATM transactions early on Thursday morning. The outage caused its customers to be unable to withdraw, deposit or transfer money with the machines. To have bank tellers handle their transactions in person, they were forced to wait for a long time in line at its branches or postpone their transactions.

The bank has not disclosed how many customers were affected, but it just experienced a similar incident last month. The latest disruption occurred while it was still investigating the cause of the previous outage. All ATMs are now back in operation, nine hours after the system went down.

To:	Amisha Wati
From:	Panuta Bayu
Date:	Friday, October 6
Subject:	Online Banking

Dear Amisha,

I'm sorry for interrupting you during your vacation, but I have something to tell you. I had trouble paying the rent of our shop and other bills yesterday. I entered the bank at 2:30 P.M. as usual, but it took about two hours to complete the payments there. Those who couldn't use ATMs rushed into the bank and I had to wait much longer than usual. Of course, I didn't have to pay them yesterday, but I did it just to be on the safe side because one of the payments is due on Monday. This kind of trouble is a first for me, but if the same type of problem happens and we can't make our payments, we should consider some alternatives.

Why don't we make use of an Internet banking service? Not only would it help us transact our business round-the-clock, but it would also offer other advantages. Let's discuss it next Monday.

Regards,

Panuta Bayu

1. What information is given in the article?

   (A) A period of service disruption

   (B) The cause of an outage

   (C) Customer directories

   (D) A list of ATM locations

2. What is indicated about Tates?

   (A) It is currently understaffed.

   (B) It investigates its potential customer base.

   (C) It failed to supply electricity.

   (D) It has not announced the extent of the damage.

3. In the article, the word "transfer" in paragraph 1, line 3, is closest in meaning to

   (A) change

   (B) send

   (C) relocate

   (D) move

4. What is indicated about Mr. Bayu?

   (A) He sometimes fails to pay by the due date.

   (B) He did not encounter the Tates problem a month ago.

   (C) He suggests to Ms. Wati that they merge with a bank.

   (D) He has worked as a technical advisor at Tates.

5. What will Ms. Wati most likely do next week?

   (A) Cancel a vacation

   (B) Inquire about an ATM malfunction

   (C) Contact a property company

   (D) Review banking services and benefits

Unit 14

Production & Logistics

~ing 形

このユニットでは、製造や物流に関する英語表現を学びながら、TOEIC® L&R の Part 1・Part 4・Part 5・Part 6 の出題形式を学習します。

Key Words & Phrases

A 音声を聞いて、1～20の語句とその意味を確認しましょう。その後、ペアで問題を出し合いましょう。

DL 099　CD3-44

1. pack	～を梱包する	☐☐	**10.** operate	～を操作する	☐☐
2. stack	～を積み重ねる	☐☐	**11.** (raw) material	原材料	☐☐
3. warehouse	倉庫	☐☐	**12.** monitor	～を監視する	☐☐
storage		☐☐	**13.** improve	～を改良する	☐☐
4. inspect	～を点検する	☐☐	**14.** ship	～を出荷する	☐☐
5. production	製造	☐☐	dispatch		☐☐
manufacturing		☐☐	**15.** location	位置、場所	☐☐
6. factory	工場	☐☐	**16.** retailer	小売業者	☐☐
plant		☐☐	**17.** component	部品	☐☐
7. automobile	自動車	☐☐	**18.** logistics	物流	☐☐
8. assemble	～を組み立てる	☐☐	**19.** courier	宅配業者	☐☐
9. industrial	産業の	☐☐	**20.** manufacturer	製造業者、メーカー	
					☐☐

B 音声を聞いて、語を書き入れましょう。

DL 100　CD3-45 ～ CD3-47

1. The (①   ) carefully delivered those packages containing precision
(②   ).

2. Ms. Sato is (①   ) and sorting the products in the logistics
(②   ).

3. Their (①   ) process of (②   )
automobiles is being monitored by some cameras in the factory.

Listening Build Up

Point 風景写真問題では、人物描写を除外する

人物が写ってない風景写真問題では、音声で読まれる選択肢の主語が全て異なる形が約95%を占めます。本ユニットでは人物が写っていない風景写真で、選択肢の主語が全て異なる形の問題を練習します。人物を描写する英文や、人物の存在を匂わせる英文は、避けるようにしましょう。

Q 音声を聞いて空所を埋めた後、写真に合う説明文を(A)～(D)から選びましょう。

(A) Some (　　　　　　) are (　　　　　　　　　) products in the workshop.
(B) Many cartons are (　　　　　　　　) in the (　　　　　　　).
(C) Many boxes are being (　　　　　　　) out of (　　　　　　).
(D) Some (　　　　　　　　) are inspecting the (　　　　　　　).

Point 図表問題の「先読み」と心の準備②

グラフタイプの図表問題では、数値や割合を中心に話が進められることが多いので、数値や割合をよく見ておきましょう。グラフタイプの問題の約半数は、数値や割合が最も高い、あるいは最も低い項目を選ばせる問題になっていますが、数値や割合の変化が著しい項目を問われる場合もあるので、併せてチェックしておきましょう。また、フロアマップや駐車場などの図表問題では、位置関係の把握が重要なので、図表を先読みする際に目印となる部屋や建造物の位置などを必ず確認しておきましょう。

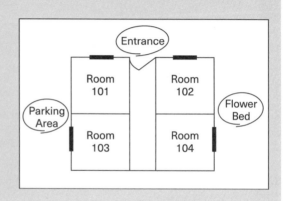

Q 説明文を聞いて空所を埋めた後、設問の答えを(A)と(B)から選びましょう。

Questions 1 and 2 refer to the following (1. _____) and graph.

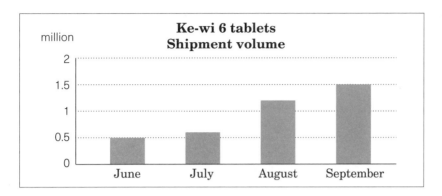

W: Thanks to your great (2. _____), our new Ke-wi 6 tablets have been (3. _____) quite well. Especially in the month we started advertising on social networking sites, they got popular among students, and the shipment (4. _____) increased remarkably. I'm sorry I may ask you to work overtime for a while to increase production. You will be given (5. _____) to apply for leave after the busy season.

1. Who most likely are the listeners?
   (A) Factory workers
   (B) University students

2. Look at the graphic. When did the advertisement most likely start?
   (A) June
   (B) August

Listening Try Out

Select the one statement that best describes what you see in the picture.

(A)　(B)　(C)　(D)

Listen to the talk while looking at the graphic and select the best response to each question.

Entrance

1. Who most likely is the listener?

　(A) An office worker　　　　(C) A construction worker

　(B) A truck driver　　　　　(D) A security guard

2. Look at the graphic. Where should the listener park a vehicle?

　(A) Space 1　　　　　　　　(C) Space 3

　(B) Space 2　　　　　　　　(D) Space 4

3. According to the speaker, what will happen next week?

　(A) New maps will be distributed to their customers.

　(B) Their parking lot will be closed.

　(C) Pavement construction will be conducted.

　(D) All the trucks and machines will be inspected.

Reading Build Up

~ing 形

→ 空所に適切な日本語を書き入れましょう。

(1.　　　　) 分詞「〜している」は、名詞の前後に置いて、the man **operating** a crane のように名詞を修飾したり、〈be動詞 + ~ing〉の形で The man is **operating** a crane. のように (2.　　　　) 形を作ったりします。

(3.　　　　) 詞「〜すること」には動作を名詞化する働きがあります。**Operating** a crane is difficult. のように (4.　　　) 語になったり、The man enjoyed **operating** a crane. のように他動詞の (5.　　　　) 語になったり、His job is **operating** a crane. のように補語になったり、The man is tired of **operating** a crane. のように (6.　　　　) 詞の目的語になったりします。

分詞構文は、~ing の中に (7.　　　　) 詞の意味を伴うもので、「〜している時」(時)、「〜なので」(原因・理由)、「もし〜なら」(条件)、「〜だけれども」(譲歩)、「〜しながら」(付帯状況)、「そして〜」(結果) の6つの訳し方があります。

Part 5

Point ~ing 形の区別は、構造だけでなく意味も大事に

分詞構文はほとんどの場合、コンマで文が区切られているので分かりやすいですが、現在分詞と動名詞は見分けにくいため、動詞に注目しながら構造を確認して、意味を考えましょう。

Q 文を完成させるのに、正しい語を選びましょう。

1. The supervisor is (monitoring / monitored) the manufacturing process in the control room.

2. An urgent task for us is to achieve a low price by (improving / improvement) materials and techniques.

3. (Operating / Operation) the forklift, you need to pay more attention to what is around you.

Point 順序を表す語に注目

First、Secondly [Also / Next / Then / Moreover]、Finally などの順序を表す接続副詞は、それ自体が問われる場合と、接続副詞が解答のヒントとなる場合とがあります。「最初に」や「また」のような表現を見つけたら、何と何を並列させているのかを考える習慣を身に付けましょう。

Q 文書を完成させるのに、正しい語句や文を選びましょう。

Questions 1-3 refer to the following notice.

To Staff:

We have some reports about shipping to wrong addresses. To avoid
1.(misdelivering / to misdeliver) items, QR code labels are being introduced.
First, when items arrive at our warehouse, print QR code labels and stick them
to items. Then, put the items with labels on the proper shelves. Make sure to
scan the labels of both the items and their locations. Finally, when 2.(picks /
picking) up items to ship to retailers, scan the QR codes on packing lists and
shipments. 3.(They are extremely expensive / Thanks in advance for your
cooperation).

Reading Try Out

Select the best answer to complete the sentence.

1. Daniel advised the engineer ------- electric components to check the joint from the left side.

(A) assemble   (B) assembles   (C) assembling   (D) assembled

2. Mr. Abdula decided to put off ------- the latest model of a press machine at his factory because he heard it often stops working.

(A) install   (B) installing   (C) installed   (D) installation

3. ------- packages at a logistics center, Jessica's glove got caught on the edge of the conveyor belt.

(A) To sort   (B) Sorting   (C) To sorting   (D) Sorted

4. Customers can download the ------- manual from the support page.

(A) produce   (B) product   (C) production   (D) productivity

5. Once our order has been ------- from their warehouse, we usually receive an e-mail containing our tracking number from their courier.

(A) discounted   (B) dismissed   (C) dispatched   (D) disturbed

Questions 1-4 refer to the following article.

An Indian manufacturer, Toby Packing Systems, is raising the prices of all its products by 5% in October. Although it has been affected by the rising cost of raw materials and transportation, it has searched for various ways to reduce production costs. Despite its -------, it finally failed to keep prices lower than its
1.
competitors.

As a leading company in the industry, Toby Packing Systems specializes in ------- single-use plastic bags and trays. Its products are much in demand.
2.
First, it is proud of the quality of its products. For example, the plastic bags for vegetables have better ventilation and more strength than those of any other company. -------, it can deal with an order of custom-made products promptly.
3.
-------. However, the decision to hike prices may lead its sales to second place.
4.

1. (A) efforts
   (B) recession
   (C) vehicles
   (D) relocation

2. (A) manufacture
   (B) manufacturer
   (C) manufactures
   (D) manufacturing

3. (A) For that reason
   (B) Instead
   (C) Additionally
   (D) On the other hand

4. (A) These offerings will be available after they have been examined.
   (B) The wider range of colors, sizes, and types is highly recognized nationwide.
   (C) It will shut down its plants for the annual inspection next month.
   (D) The retailers are not allowed to return them.

Unit 15

Research and Development & ICT

関係詞

このユニットでは、研究開発やICTに関する英語表現を学びながら、TOEIC® L&RのPart 2・Part 3・Part 5・Part 7の出題形式を学習します。

Key Words & Phrases

A 音声を聞いて、1〜20の語句とその意味を確認しましょう。その後、ペアで問題を出し合いましょう。

DL 107　CD3-58

1. lab(oratory)	研究室	☐☐	**11.** design	〜を設計する	☐☐
2. experiment	実験	☐☐	**12.** innovative	革新的な	☐☐
3. specify	〜を詳細に述べる	☐☐	**13.** disposable	使い捨ての	☐☐
4. install	〜をインストールする	☐☐	**14.** durable	耐性のある、丈夫な	☐☐
5. laptop	ノートパソコン	☐☐	**15.** scrutinize	〜を詳細に調べる	☐☐
6. reboot	(〜を)再起動する	☐☐	**16.** prototype	試作品	☐☐
7. R&D	研究開発	☐☐	**17.** equipment	機材、設備	☐☐
(Research and Development)			**18.** improvement	改良、改善	☐☐
8. microscope	顕微鏡	☐☐	**19.** facility	施設	☐☐
9. performance	性能	☐☐	**20.** expiration	期限切れ	☐☐
10. engineer	技師	☐☐			

B 音声を聞いて、語を書き入れましょう。

DL 108　CD3-59 〜 CD3-61

1. The laboratory where Dr. Tsukuda works (①　　　　　　　) the polished surface with a high-resolution electron (②　　　　　　　).

2. Our (①　　　　　　) department developed an (②　　　　　　　) method in which we can reuse plastic waste to construct durable roads.

3. The (①　　　　　　), to which Ms. Garcia installed a new program, started (②　　　　　　).

Listening Build Up

Point 平叙文への応答問題は、一つ一つの選択肢を吟味する

平叙文はさまざまな形で返答することが可能です。例えば、「コピー機が壊れています」という発言に対して、①「さっき、業者に電話しました」(報告)、②「それは困りますね」(感想)、③「どんな症状ですか」(質問)、④「外でコピーしてきましょうか」(申し出)、⑤「買い替えを検討しませんか」(提案)のいずれも、応答として成立します。最も自然なやり取りが成立するものを選びましょう。

Q 音声を聞いて空所を埋めた後、適切な応答文を(A)〜(C)から選びましょう。

1. I (　　　　　　) not to have locked the lab door.

  (A) You (　　　　　　) go back immediately.

  (B) This is the key I was (　　　　　　) for.

  (C) I (　　　　　　) the door black.

2. The experiment we conducted last week was a huge (　　　　　　).

  (A) Could you specify (　　　　　　) how?

  (B) I know the (　　　　　　).

  (C) He is one of the most (　　　　　　) people.

Point 音声の変化に慣れよう

自然な速度で話す時、一つ一つの単語をはっきり発音しないため、さまざまな音声変化が起こります。check it out が「チェキダウト」に聞こえたり(連結)、right now が「ゥライナウ」に聞こえたり(脱落)します。また、want to が wanna「ワナ」、going to が gonna「ガナ」と発音される(短縮)こともあります。発音練習をする時には音声変化に注意してリピートするようにし、音声の変化に慣れましょう。

Q 会話文を聞いて空所を埋めた後、設問の答えを(A)と(B)から選びましょう。

Questions 1 and 2 refer to the following conversation.

W: Thank you for (¹.　　　　　　) Fine Systems' customer center. How may I help you?

M: I installed your application on my (².　　　　　　), but now it's constantly freezing.

W: I see … Did you try (³.　　　　　　) your computer?

M: Yes, but nothing has changed.

W: OK. Let me check the (4.   ) conditions. Can you please open the Task Manager on your computer?

M: I'm going to do that now.

1. What most likely is the woman's occupation?
   (A) A software designer
   (B) A customer service rep

2. What does the woman ask the man to do?
   (A) Operate a computer
   (B) Read a manual

Listening Try Out

Listen to the question or statement and the three responses. Then select the best response to the question or statement.

1. (A) (B) (C)
2. (A) (B) (C)
3. (A) (B) (C)

Listen to the conversation while looking at the graphic and select the best response to each question.

Manufacturer	Price
Thermotechno	$205,000
Adamas Scientific	$170,000
Optimax	$149,000
Central Instrument	$115,000

1. What division do the speakers most likely work in?
   (A) HR
   (B) Accounting
   (C) R&D
   (D) Sales

2. Look at the graphic. Whose product is the man going to order?
   (A) Thermotechno
   (B) Adamas Scientific
   (C) Optimax
   (D) Central Instrument

3. What does the woman say about Central Instrument?
   (A) It may be a start-up.
   (B) It can reduce its price.
   (C) She has used its products before.
   (D) She worked in its laboratory.

Reading Build Up

関係詞

—•空所に適切な日本語や英語を書き入れましょう。

関係代名詞は、その直前にある（1.　　　　　）詞と呼ばれる名詞句を修飾する働きをします。次の関係代名詞の表を埋めましょう。

先行詞	主格	所有格	目的格（省略可）
人	who	(2.　　　　　)	who(m)
動物や物	which	whose	(3.　　　　　)
人、動物や物	(4.　　　　　)	——	that

関係代名詞のwhatは、what she said「彼女が言った（5.　　　　　）」やwhat he has「彼が持っているもの」のように漠然とした物・事を表すのに使われ、先行詞がありません。

関係副詞は、関係代名詞と同じように先行詞を修飾する働きをしますが、先行詞が「場所」の場合は (6.　　　　　)、先行詞が「時」の場合はwhen、先行詞が「理由」の場合は (7.　　　　) を用います。

Part 5

Point **関係代名詞と関係副詞と接続詞の違いを再確認しよう**

関係代名詞 who、which、that には先行詞があり、関係代名詞の後ろは不完全文が来ます。関係代名詞 what には先行詞がなく、関係代名詞の後ろは不完全文が来ます。関係副詞 where や when には先行詞がある場合もない場合もあり、関係副詞の後ろは完全文が来ます。選択肢には接続詞が混ざっている場合も多いので、空所前の先行詞の有無と空所後の構造に加えて、意味も考えるようにしましょう。

Q 文を完成させるのに、正しい語を選びましょう。

1. Shantanu is an excellent engineer (who / which) designed and created the innovative software.

2. The researchers are developing technology to visualize (that / what) comes to our minds from our brain activity.

3. The laboratory building (where / when) our R&D department is situated was built in 1987.

Part 7

 トリプルパッセージ問題の設問設定

トリプルパッセージの問題には設問が5つありますが、そのうち約2問は2つの文書を参照しなければならないクロスレファレンス問題です。まずは単独の文書から答えが出せる設問から始めましょう。トリプルパッセージの問題は、7分程度での解答を目指しましょう。

Q 3つの文書を読んで、設問の答えを(A)と(B)から選びましょう。

Questions 1-3 refer to the following Web page, memo, and invoice.

https://www.omnisup/int/gloves　　_ □ ✕

OmniSup Ltd.

Exam Gloves

Polyethylene Gloves (G13)	**Vinyl Gloves (G14)**
Our thinnest disposable polyethylene gloves with a thickness of just 0.03 mm.	Durable, disposable PVC gloves, 0.07 mm thick. Powdered for easy wearing and removal.
Powder-free Vinyl Gloves (G15)	**Hybrid Powder-free Gloves (G16)**
Durable, disposable PVC gloves, 0.07 mm thick. Powder-free and latex-free. Ideal for those with latex allergies.	Powder-free disposable gloves made of a combination of vinyl and nitrile. No need to worry for those with latex allergies. *Discontinued!
Nitrile Gloves (G17)	
With a thickness of 0.13 mm, these are our firmest gloves. They can be worn in layers due to their resistance to friction.	

MEMO

To: All staff in the R&D Department
From: William Davis, lead researcher
Date: March 6

Our monthly order for research supplies has changed slightly. The gloves for latex allergies have been newly replaced with another product, the Powder-free Vinyl Gloves. This is the first time we have ordered them, but those with latex allergies can use them safely. The rest of the regular order remains unchanged.

OmniSup Ltd.
Invoice

Address: 592 Claryon Street, Fairfax, Virginia
Phone: 756-932-5894

Purchased by: Colorado Research Labs Inc.
Address: 18352 Farnham Way, Albion, Colorado
Phone: 833-492-5886

Order number: 15SPC397-661
Purchase date: March 18
Shipping date: March 21

Item	Description	Quantity	Unit Cost	Total Price
G14	Vinyl Gloves	8	$32	$256
G15	Powder-free Vinyl Gloves	12	$34	$408

	Sub-total:	$664.00
	7% sales tax:	$46.48
	Delivery:	$0.00
	Total Charges:	**$710.48**

1. According to the Web page, which is true about the products?

   (A) Discounts are available for bulk purchases.

   (B) A certain item is no longer available.

2. What is the main purpose of the memo?

   (A) To inform the staff of a change in their order

   (B) To announce a price increase of a product

3. How much will Colorado Research Labs pay for the newly ordered product?

   (A) $256

   (B) $408

Reading Try Out

Part 5

Select the best answer to complete the sentence.

1. Our team is working on developing glass fiber reinforced concrete ------- will be durable against heat.
(A) who   (B) whose   (C) what   (D) that

2. Unitech Ltd. has entered the pre-production phase ------- they will scrutinize their prototype before mass production.
(A) which   (B) what   (C) when   (D) where

3. Most modern people just can't imagine the days in ------- they lived without their smartphones.
(A) which   (B) what   (C) when   (D) where

4. That's why your lithium metal battery has a lot of room for ------- at the moment.
(A) assignment   (B) equipment   (C) improvement   (D) settlement

5. M&M Biopharma is planning to expand its experimental -------, which has played a leading role in developing its vaccines and medicines.
(A) curiosity   (B) facility   (C) heredity   (D) priority

Part 7

Questions **1-5** refer to the following notice, schedule, and e-mail.

Notice

- From April 5 to May 10 the clean room will be upgraded.
- The clean room will be unavailable due to the construction, so please make sure not to schedule any experiments. During this time use the west wing of the building for non-experiment related work.
- You will be issued a temporary employee ID card to access the building, as your current employee ID card will not be valid during the construction period. Please come to the General Affairs office in the Campbell Building to get your temporary employee ID.

- A training session for the updated clean room will be held following the construction. All employees are required to attend. Please assemble at the change room in a clean room suit five minutes before the specified time.
- If you cannot attend the training session on the scheduled date, you will have to watch an online video. Please inquire at the HR department for the passcode.
- If you have any questions, please contact Clarence Carter at HR.

Training Session Schedule

Date	Training Team	Time
May 12	Team T	2:00–3:30 P.M.
May 13	Team K	2:00–3:30 P.M.
May 14	Team M	4:00–5:30 P.M.
May 15	Team P	2:00–3:30 P.M.

To:	Clarence Carter
From:	Sharon Clarkson
Date:	Tuesday, May 9
Subject:	Passcode

Mr. Carter,

I will be unable to attend the clean room training session on May 13. I have a meeting scheduled in the afternoon for a joint development project with Aurora University. After that, I have another meeting with Wallace Industries and a distributor that handle raw materials for us. Please send the passcode for the online video.

Sharon Clarkson

1. What is one purpose of the notice?

    (A) To encourage staff to participate in an event

    (B) To present research results

    (C) To notify employees of their ID cards' expiration

    (D) To announce the location of a video recording

2. What is indicated about the clean room?

    (A) Recording equipment has been set up.

    (B) Small experiments can be conducted.

    (C) It is going to be renovated.

    (D) It is located in the west wing.

3. What is suggested about the training sessions?

    (A) The length of a session varies depending on the date.

    (B) They will be held twice a day during the construction period.

    (C) The staff of Team T must gather in the change room at 1:45 P.M.

    (D) Available employees must attend at least one from May 12 to 15.

4. What problem does Ms. Clarkson have?

    (A) She lost her employee ID card.

    (B) The training schedule conflicts with her schedule.

    (C) The joint project with Aurora University might be cancelled.

    (D) Wallace Industries' raw materials are unavailable.

5. Which team does Ms. Clarkson belong to?

    (A) Team T

    (B) Team K

    (C) Team M

    (D) Team P

このシールをはがすと
CheckLink 利用のための
「教科書固有番号」が
記載されています。

一度はがすと元に戻すことは
できませんのでご注意下さい。

4207 CLIMB HIGH TO
THE TOEIC® L&R TEST

◀ここからはがして下さい

本書にはCD（別売）があります

CLIMB HIGH TO THE TOEIC® L&R TEST

TOEIC® L&R テスト　高みへのステップ

2024年1月20日　初版第1刷発行
2024年2月20日　初版第2刷発行

著　者　　安丸　雅子
　　　　　渡邉　晶子
　　　　　十時　　康
　　　　　Andrew Zitzmann
　　　　　濱　奈々恵

発行者　　福岡　正人

発行所　　株式会社　金星堂

（〒101-0051）東京都千代田区神田神保町 3-21
　　　Tel　（03）3263-3828（営業部）
　　　　　　（03）3263-3997（編集部）
　　　Fax　（03）3263-0716
　　　https://www.kinsei-do.co.jp

編集担当　池田恭子・四條雪菜　　　　　　　Printed in Japan
印刷所・製本所／三美印刷株式会社

ISBN978-4-7647-4207-9　C1082